EARTH SQUAD

Written by **ALEXANDRA ZISSU**

Illustrated by **NHUNG LÊ**

RP|KIDS
PHILADELPHIA

Running Press Kids
Hachette Book Group
1290 Avenue of the Americas, New York, NY 10104
www.runningpress.com/rpkids
@RP_Kids

Printed in Singapore

First Edition: March 2021

Published by Running Press Kids, an imprint of Perseus Books, LLC,
a subsidiary of Hachette Book Group, Inc. The Running Press Kids
name and logo is a trademark of the Hachette Book Group.

The Hachette Speakers Bureau provides a wide range of authors for
speaking events. To find out more, go to www.hachettespeakersbureau.com
or call (866) 376-6591.

The publisher is not responsible for websites (or their content)
that are not owned by the publisher.

Cover and interior illustrations by Nhung Lê.
Print book cover and interior design by Marissa Raybuck.

Library of Congress Control Number: 2020937347

ISBNs: 9780762499212 (hardcover),
9780762499205 (ebook)

COS

10 9 8 7 6 5 4 3 2 1

TO NATURE

CONTENTS

INTRODUCTION

The following pages contain the amazing stories of fifty inspiring people from all walks of life, from all over the world, who have many different kinds of jobs. They are doctors and protestors and politicians, scientists and ship captains and activists, journalists and actors and farmers, artists and singers and architects. These global citizens range from young to old—and some of them lived before you were even born. They all have one thing in common: they have devoted their lives to loving and protecting our shared home, the wondrous and beautiful planet earth. As you read about them and their work, you may find yourself feeling inspired to join the Earth Squad. Great! That's why there are suggested actions on every page—real things you can do to make a difference right away. Protecting the earth takes all of us. Consider this your invitation!

> Throughout the book, you'll see some words in **bold**. These are important environmental terms—their definitions are in the Glossary on page 152, in case you don't already know what they mean!

GRETA THUNBERG B. 2003

Climate & Environmental Activist

When she was sixteen, Greta Thunberg was named *Time* magazine's 2019 Person of the Year. It's a really big deal for anyone to be given this awesome acknowledgment, especially someone so young. Greta is the Swedish activist who decided to strike for the climate outside the Swedish Parliament instead of going to school one Friday in 2018. That day, she stood alone. But she came back every week, and slowly others joined her, and the Fridays for Future movement was born. Within a year, there were millions of people striking with Greta all over the world, and she began speaking regularly at international gatherings like the UN Climate Action Summit. Since then, Greta has met with the pope and spoken at the US Congress, the World Economic Forum, and the British Parliament. This is totally amazing for anyone, but especially a teenager!

Wherever she speaks, Greta's message is consistent: She demands that people listen to climate scientists and immediately take the urgent action needed to reverse growth in **greenhouse gas** emissions and avoid catastrophic **climate change**. She also calls for **climate justice** and equity, which in part means having rich countries reduce their emissions faster than poorer ones, so citizens in poorer countries have a chance to improve their standard of living and access basic needs like roads, electricity, and even clean drinking water. Not everyone has these, which isn't fair.

Although there are many youth activists and climate researchers with similar messages, Greta has struck a global nerve. Her work has earned her a very important Nobel Peace Prize nomination and France's prestigious Prix Liberté. She has turned down some awards, including financial ones, because she says the climate movement doesn't need more prizes. "What we need is for our rulers and politicians to listen to the research," she says again and again. Politicians claim they are listening—to her. "When you are a leader and every week you have young people demonstrating with such a message, you cannot remain neutral," French president Emmanuel Macron has told *Time*. US president Donald Trump regularly insults her on social media.

3

Greta was eight when she first learned about **global warming**. It horrified her how little was being done about something so serious. We're nearing a point of no return because of how much carbon we release into the atmosphere. She couldn't believe people were—and are—living as if we have endless resources, as if species weren't going extinct daily. At eleven, Greta fell into a climate depression. She spoke little and ate less. Her parents took steps to reduce their own emissions, including giving up flying, which was how her mother, an opera singer, traveled to her performances. Today Greta travels by train, not airplane, and famously crossed the ocean to North America on a zero-emissions boat to bring global awareness to the carbon footprint of plane travel.

Activism has helped Greta's depression. On September 20, 2019, an estimated 4 million people took part in a global climate strike, asking world leaders to act while there's still time. It's clear Greta's Fridays for Future movement will continue to grow. The question remains whether her outrage, frustration, and proactive anger will result in meaningful change while there's still a chance. We already have the solutions we need. Today's leaders won't always be in charge; soon Greta and her fellow student strikers will be voting age, but by then it might be too late. As Greta says, the science has been crystal clear for thirty years: the world is changing whether we like it or not, and our future depends on acting now.

GRETA HAS ASPERGER'S, a syndrome that's on the autism spectrum. People with it often have a deep interest in specific topics. Greta describes Asperger's as a "gift" because it helps her see the climate crisis in black and white and to think outside the box.

GRETA'S FIRST BOOK, *No One Is Too Small to Make a Difference,* is a great collection of speeches she has given across the globe.

ACT LIKE GRETA

Strike! Speak truth to power! "I think that if a few children can get headlines all over the world just by not going to school for a few weeks, imagine what we all could do together if we wanted to," says Greta.

WANGARI MAATHAI

B. 1940–D. 2011

Nobel Peace Prize Winner & Mother of Trees

Planting a tree is a small and simple act. It's also how Wangari Maathai started the Green Belt Movement in 1977 in Kenya, Africa. People in Kenya were cutting down forests to clear land and develop it for other uses. But a tree is part of a complicated and amazing system, and this **deforestation** was setting off a chain of reactions and causing food and water shortages. Wild animals also lost their natural habitat and food sources. To help fix these problems, Wangari asked women in the community to plant trees and take back their land. One tree soon became many. The movement took off and eventually resulted in more than 51 million trees planted! These trees not only helped the environment by rebuilding wild animals' habitats, but they also benefitted the broader community they were a part of. Trees improve the soil for growing food. As the Green Belt Movement's women fought for justice and repaired their land, they learned valuable skills and earned money for their families.

Wangari was a trailblazer all her life. In the small rural village where she grew up, her parents were farmers and chose to send her to school. This was unusual for girls at that time in Kenya. Even then, when it was nearly unheard of for a girl, she wanted to be a scientist. She was a good student and won a scholarship to go to college in the United States, where she also earned a graduate degree in biological sciences. Back home in Kenya in 1971, she became the first woman in East Africa to earn a doctorate degree! A few years later, she became a professor and the first woman to chair a department at the University of Nairobi.

Over the years, Wangari has won many awards and international praise for her innovation and dedication to saving the planet. She was even given the nickname "Mama Miti"—mother of trees. Still, her work was often a struggle. Because she spoke out about political issues, she was arrested—and even beaten—more than once. But when the Kenyan government changed, she was able to join its Parliament in 2002. She was also named the assistant minister

5

of environment and natural resources. In 2009, the UN secretary-general appointed her a UN messenger of peace, focusing on the environment and climate change.

Wangari was the first African woman to receive the Nobel Peace Prize, a really important award given to people who do something extraordinary for the good of all humankind. She won it in 2004 for "**sustainable** development, democracy, and peace."

Unfortunately, Mama Miti lost her life to ovarian cancer in 2011. She was only seventy-one and surely had so much more to share with the world. Her beautiful legacy lives on with her children, grandchildren, and the untold numbers of trees around the world that she helped plant or protect, all of which are doing their part to this day to fight the **climate crisis** by cleaning the air, enriching the soil, and building community.

· ·

WANGARI WROTE FOUR books: *The Green Belt Movement, Unbowed: A Memoir, The Challenge for Africa,* and *Replenishing the Earth.* She is also the subject of many books and even a documentary film, *Taking Root: The Vision of Wangari Maathai.*

PEOPLE STILL REPEAT so many of Wangari's inspirational quotes today, especially on social media. Here's one: "We all share one planet and are one humanity; there is no escaping this reality."

ACT LIKE MAMA MITI

· ·

Put your hands in the dirt and plant trees. The simple act of planting a seed plus many likeminded people can make a revolution—fighting environmental harm and poverty.

ERIN BROCKOVICH

B. 1960

Consumer Advocate & Legal Clerk

When Erin Brockovich was a kid in Lawrence, Kansas, her parents believed she could do anything—as long as she focused her energy. When she grew up, she did just that.

As a single mother of three young kids and in need of a job, Erin became a legal researcher for a lawyer named Edward Masry. Working at his law firm, she discovered that California's largest energy supplier, Pacific Gas and Electric (PG&E), was polluting the water in a desert town called Hinkley. They had a compressor station there, which is basically a large facility that helps move natural gas from one location to another. PG&E lied to the people who lived in Hinkley, saying their water was safe when it actually contained harmful chemicals from the compressor station. Starting in the 1950s, the company poisoned residents of Hinkley and made them sick, kids included. For many decades, PG&E offered to buy their houses from them and to pay for them to go see doctors that the company hired. Those doctors also lied, telling the people that their illnesses were not related to the "safe" water.

In fact, the water was contaminated by a chemical called hexavalent chromium. PG&E was using this chemical to prevent rust in equipment called cooling towers, then dumping it in wastewater ponds. These ponds are always supposed to be lined to prevent whatever is in them from seeping out and getting into the groundwater. But PG&E's ponds didn't have liners.

Erin isn't a lawyer, and she had no training in how to do investigative work. But she cared deeply about these sick families. So she focused her energy and went door to door in Hinkley, gaining people's trust, talking to them about their illnesses (which included many kinds of cancer), and gathering evidence to build a legal case against PG&E. She obtained records of the local water and took samples from wells. She interviewed experts about hexavalent chromium to learn what it can do to people's health.

There were many ups and downs along the way, and getting this case together took time. But Erin's persistence and dedication paid off. In 1996, PG&E settled the lawsuit for a whopping $333 million! The company had to pay more than six hundred people who lived in Hinkley for poisoning their water. This settlement was the largest award in this kind of lawsuit—called a direct-action lawsuit—in US history, and it sent a message to all large companies that they should not poison people or lie as they conduct business—ever.

9

And yet many companies continue to contaminate the environment with chemicals and lie about it, even though it makes people sick, and even though they can get caught. That's why Erin is still busy exposing the truth about groundwater **contamination** and other environmental health concerns to this day!

. . . .

THE PG&E COVER-UP was made into a blockbuster movie called *Erin Brockovich*. The actress Julia Roberts played Erin and won a 2001 Academy Award for her performance.

THE POPULATION OF Hinkley today is very small. Over time, PG&E bought most of the homes there and demolished them. Cleaning up all of the hexavalent chromium is slow work. By one estimate, only 80 percent of the cleanup of contamination that started back in the 1950s will be complete by 2032. Hinkley is still polluted, and the people who live there remain in danger.

ACT LIKE ERIN

. . . .

Be a voice for people who can't speak up for themselves. Make a difference in your own backyard. Organize your community to expose injustice. Tell the truth. Fight for your neighbors' health as if it were your own.

XIUHTEZCATL MARTINEZ

Climate Activist & Hip-Hop Artist

Young people play an important role in social change movements. Xiuhtezcatl (pronounced Shoe-Tez-Caht) Martinez has been an environmental leader his whole life, protesting all over the United States and abroad since age six! At nine, he joined a movement to ban pesticides in parks in his hometown of Boulder, Colorado. By eleven, he was fighting fracking, an environmentally destructive way of removing natural gas from underground rock, as youth director of Earth Guardians, an organization his mother founded before he was born. At thirteen, he won a community service award from President Obama. By fourteen, he was speaking at the United Nations. He's an inspiration and proof that anyone can have a real impact, even if you aren't yet old enough to vote.

Xiuhtezcatl uses many different strategies to spread awareness and pressure politicians about the climate crisis. In 2015, he joined twenty other youth activists and sued the US government for failing to protect the atmosphere for future generations. This landmark lawsuit didn't stop President Obama from appointing him to his youth council!

Xiuhtezcatl is of Indigenous Mexican descent on his father's side; his people are the Mashika, Aztecs originally from Mexico City. His heritage has influenced him—he says protecting the earth and lifting up his generation is his spiritual duty. Kids today have inherited a future of drought, hurricanes, storms, wildfires, and tornadoes. Right now communities are already suffering, animals are going extinct, and island nations are disappearing because of a rise in sea level brought on by the climate crisis. Xiuhtezcatl's response is to educate people about the climate. He makes a point of referring to our current situation as a crisis, not just change or warming. And he shares solutions—the current technologies that can help us move away from destructive **fossil fuels**.

Xiuhtezcatl wishes the media would pay attention to all of the activists focusing today on the climate crisis, including young people, and especially Black, Brown, and Indigenous people. The activists who receive the most attention in newspapers and on television tend to

be white, and they're usually men. This doesn't mean that, say, Al Gore (see page 77) or even Greta Thunberg aren't doing critically important work. They are! But there are others, too, who deserve recognition for their roles in the climate movement. Xiuhtezcatl wants to connect other Indigenous and Latinx youth to this movement, especially because the climate crisis affects people of color the most. He knows that his is the last generation with a fighting chance to keep greenhouse gas emissions in the atmosphere at a safe level and to hold off the worst effects of climate disaster. Xiuhtezcatl believes strongly that the climate is the most important issue of our time and that every single one of us has a role to play in fighting for it. Join him!

XIUHTEZCATL IS ALSO a hip-hop artist who works with his siblings. One of their records, *Generation RYSE,* has songs with titles such as "Speak for the Trees," "Return to Nature," and "Children's Rights."

WHEN XIUHTEZCATL SPOKE at the United Nations, he addressed world leaders in three languages: English, Spanish, and Nahuatl, his ancestors' native language.

ACT LIKE XIUHTEZCATL

You're never too young to protest and make noise. Find your passion, gather your friends and family, and start fighting the climate crisis and for climate justice. Start small with something local and work your way up.

BILL McKIBBEN

B. 1960

Author, Educator & Environmentalist

Journalists tell other people's stories. They're not really supposed to be a part of these stories themselves. But at some point in his work as both a writer and one of America's most important environmentalists, Bill McKibben became a key part of the story of the fight against the climate crisis, which has been a good thing for all inhabitants of the earth—and our future!

Bill grew up in the suburbs of Boston. After college, he worked as a journalist in New York City, then left the city and moved to the woods. There, he hiked, biked, swam, and generally enjoyed the natural world. He wrote about this in *The End of Nature*, the first of his many books. Published in 1989, *The End of Nature* is now a classic, as it was the first book to really alert people who aren't scientists to the fact that our planet was (and still is) warming. It has been translated into more than twenty languages. In the book, he urges people to take action against global warming by getting governments to pass environmental laws and to join international environmental agreements. He also calls on people to use **renewable energy,** like solar, instead of polluting fossil fuels.

It's now many years since Bill wrote *The End of Nature,* and the majority of people all over the world still go about their lives as if things are normal—when in fact we're in the middle of a crisis that threatens our survival. In 2008, to wake people up and spur them to take climate action, Bill founded 350.org with some friends. As an environmental organization, 350.org's main focus is inspiring a huge global movement to match the hugeness of the climate crisis: 350.org has organized over 20,000 rallies all around the world! If you've been to a climate march or action day with your school or family, chances are 350.org was involved.

Bill the writer became the great organizer of a social movement. His idea of using large-scale, nonviolent civil disobedience to create change has a long history. Women who fought for the right to vote (known as suffragists) and well-known political activists like Gandhi and Dr. Martin Luther King Jr. all led successful movements that allowed, as Bill has put it, the small and many to stand up to the mighty and few. This kind of mass protest really works! After Americans gathered in mass protest for the first Earth Day in 1970, they got real change in the form of laws that have protected us all: the Clean Air Act, the Clean Water Act, and the Endangered Species Act. Bill believes people hitting the streets all over the world today will result in similar change for the climate crisis. UN climate chief Christiana Figueres (see page 68) has said that Bill's organizing is so influential, it helped get the 2015 Paris Climate Agreement signed.

One big difference between the climate crisis and past political issues like the right to vote is timing. With climate, we have a deadline to reduce emissions before it's too late. Can we make real change fast enough? Bill is betting on a climate movement powerful enough to go against the fossil fuel industry. Making it happen will take every single person doing their part, including you.

BILL HAS WON many important awards over the years for his environmental work, including the Right Livelihood Award, the Gandhi Peace Award, and the Thomas Merton Award. He's also been given honorary degrees from eighteen colleges and universities.

A NEW SPECIES of woodland gnat found by biologists was named after Bill in 2014. It's called *Megophthalmidia mckibbeni*.

ACT LIKE BILL

Make signs. There are now young people leading demonstrations all over the world for climate action—not just Greta Thunberg, but hundreds of thousands of young people. And every demonstration works best when there are some really clever signs, like: *We're Skipping Our Lessons to Teach You One!*

ALEXANDRA KOROLEVA

B. 1954

Environmental Campaigner & Political Refugee

Imagine living in a country where being an environmental activist can get you thrown into prison. That's a scenario Alexandra Koroleva has faced in Russia for three decades! Alexandra is the head of Ecodefense, one of Russia's oldest environmental organizations. Ecodefense does lots of different kinds of work, including opposing coal mines, deforestation, and nuclear power plants. Nuclear power is a way of producing electricity efficiently, but it is also a huge possible risk to environmental health. Renewable energy, which comes from sources that don't run out, like the sun and wind, is better for the environment.

Recently, when Ecodefense was fighting to stop construction of a new nuclear power station, the Russian government told Alexandra they would put her in jail if she didn't back off. In Russia, just being a part of the green movement is a crime. (Alexandra would argue that harming the environment is the real crime!) The government has passed laws that make it nearly impossible for organizations like Ecodefense to raise money through donations, especially from people outside of Russia. But this is how many nonprofit organizations operate: people donate money to organizations they care about and support so they can pay their staff, rent office space, and buy the things they need to do their important work. Russian laws make things so hard that many environmental activists and organizations have to stop working entirely.

Things in her homeland got so bad for Alexandra that she left Russia to seek political asylum in Germany. This means she asked German officials to let her live there because living in Russia was no longer safe for her. According to some news reports, Ecodefense is still operating in Russia—for now—even without Alexandra there in person to lead it.

Being an environmental activist is hard. But it can be so much more difficult depending on where you are born and where you live. Someone brave enough to fight the good fight in a place like Russia, putting themselves in so much danger for what they believe in, is an incredible example for all of us to use our voices and stand up for the environment. The fact

that Ecodefense and Alexandra keep at it is courageous. Just imagine how much Alexandra believes in protecting the earth and all who share it, animals and humans. She's willing to risk punishment and leave her own home to fight for us. She is a true inspiration!

· ·

RUSSIA HAS MORE land than any other country in the world, including a tremendous amount of untouched wilderness. It's also considered the world's fourth-largest polluter.

ECODEFENSE IS NOT the only organization being threatened by the Russian government. It joined nearly fifty other Russian nongovernmental organizations (NGOs) to ask the European Court of Human Rights to say the actions Russia has taken against them are illegal and unfair.

ACT LIKE ALEXANDRA
· ·

If you live in a country that allows you to protest and speak your mind publicly, take advantage of that freedom! Draw a sign and bring your friends and family to a protest. Do it for Alexandra and anyone else whose government tries to silence people demanding the right to a clean and healthy environment.

LAMYA ESSEMLALI   B. 1979

Ocean Activist & Pirate for Good

You may think pirates exist only in books and movies, but Lamya Essemlali is a real live pirate—a good one, though! She's the head of Sea Shepherd France, an organization that protects oceans and marine life. Part of Lamya's job involves traveling the oceans to confront fishing boats that are harming sea animals, sometimes illegally. It's dangerous work, but it helps save dolphins, fish, whales, and more.

Sea Shepherd is active all over the world, from Denmark to Japan to Mexico. The organization was founded in 1977 by Captain Paul Watson. Fishing for food has depleted our oceans. Although some countries have banned particularly harmful ways of fishing, not all fishing boats follow the rules. Lamya cofounded the French branch of Sea Shepherd in 2006. She estimates 90 percent of the fish sold in France wasn't fished well or comes from bad sources.

One example of bad—or "unsustainable"—fishing is trawling, which means dragging a huge net along the bottom of the ocean. A fishing boat may be searching for only one species of fish to sell, but when a net is dragged this way, it winds up catching all kinds of other sea life, too. Anything alive that's accidentally scooped up is called "bycatch," which can include turtles, sea lions, and more. Since the fishermen aren't specifically selling those for food and they don't want the bycatch, the animals can end up being killed for no reason. Some fishing boats even use nets to illegally catch protected species! This is called poaching. People do this because some protected species are worth a lot of money. Who knew fishing was so complicated?

Lamya spent most of her childhood in France far from the water. But her parents are Moroccan, and when she visited family in Morocco, which is on the coast of northern Africa, she adored the sea. She has said she always felt protective of animals as a kid, including hurt birds at the playground. She wanted to be a veterinarian when she grew up. Instead, she studied environmental science and has been sailing the oceans protecting marine animals for more than fifteen years.

There are many different kinds of organizations on a mission to protect marine life. Sea Shepherd is known for taking risks, coming up with creative and sometimes provocative

21

actions to stop people from illegal fishing and hurting the oceans in other ways. Many of the governments they are up against—like that of Japan, whose programs were violating bans on catching whales—complain that their tactics are extreme. Still, Sea Shepherd gets attention, creates change, and educates the public about the big issues facing our oceans today. Sea Shepherd has also helped save porpoise habitats in the Pacific by collecting thousands of pieces of illegal fishing gear that trap them so they can't be used and brought attention to dying dolphins along the French coast. In addition, the organization has protected many fragile species including endangered whales, basking sharks, bluefin tuna, and even seabirds.

Through her work with Sea Shepherd, Lamya has witnessed the climate crisis firsthand: our oceans are warming, and sea level is rising. As this happens, humans have become an even bigger threat to marine life. There aren't going to be enough fish left in the sea at the rate people are catching and eating them. We're also taking food away from large marine animals who depend on smaller fish for survival. Destroying this food chain is bad for everyone. Lamya believes fish are better off in the oceans than on our dinner plates, and she's doing everything she can to protect them.

"ARE YOU WILLING to risk your life to save the life of a whale?" That's a question Paul, Sea Shepherd's founder, always asks his new volunteers, including Lamya when they first met. What would you answer?

SEA SHEPHERD SAYS twelve years of action against Japan's whalers have saved 6,500 whales and that Japan's whaling quota—the amount they're legally allowed to catch—has been reduced from more than 1,000 whales per year to around 300.

ACT LIKE LAMYA

At your next meal, skip the fish and leave it for a dolphin. Overfishing is destroying the ocean and killing thousands of dolphins and whales as bycatch. Also, it's starving marine predators.

ANNIE LEONARD

B. 1964

Environmental Activist & Waste Expert

What does it take to grow up and get a job as the head of one of the world's largest environmental organizations? It helps to have a super-power! Annie Leonard, currently the head of Greenpeace USA, has a special ability to think deeply about the environmental issues that people can't even see. Founded in 1971, Greenpeace inspires people all over the world to take action for a more sustainable future. Back in 2007, Annie made a short film, *The Story of Stuff.* It's a simple but brilliant twenty-one-minute movie that shines a light on the unseen: it goes behind the scenes and shows the environmental impacts of everything we own, including where our stuff goes when we throw it away.

Annie's movie explains that there's really no such thing as "away"—trash just gets moved from our homes to somewhere else. It doesn't magically disappear. It piles up in landfills, or it winds up in our oceans, where turtles, fish, and other wildlife may eat it or get tangled in it. *The Story of Stuff* shows exactly how and why every consumer—that's all of us who shop for stuff, including you—contributes to harming our shared environment.

Even as a kid, Annie thought about waste. She grew up with a single mother and not a lot of money, so they made a point of wasting nothing. Consider for a minute all the stuff you use every single day: your toothbrush, your shoes, your couch, your pet's can of food, your backpack, your family car. Each one has an **eco-impact**—how it harms or helps the earth from the time it was made to the time it's no longer of use to you. Annie Leonard's magic is being able to make this usually invisible impact clear. How cool is that?

Her film was so widely shared that it became a project—The Story of Stuff Project—which made more short films also worth watching, including *The Story of Change.* Her original film also became a best-selling book: *The Story of Stuff: How Our Obsession with Stuff Is Trashing the Planet, Our Communities, and Our Health—and a Vision for Change.* Annie's films have educated many people about the impacts of consumerism. If we know the stories behind our stuff, we're more likely to make better choices when shopping. It also motivates us to ask our elected officials to regulate the ingredients in our stuff with stronger laws and to ask businesses to use better and more recyclable materials.

As head of Greenpeace USA, Annie has also been very influential. Greenpeace uses creative and peaceful protests to bring attention to environmental problems—and solutions!—ranging from commercial whaling to **single-use plastics** (things made to be used once, then thrown out) to deforestation. Greenpeace staff and volunteers have done everything from scaling buildings to blocking ships and trains—sometimes in polar bear or even zombie costumes—like eco-superheroes in the name of environmental justice. Annie is the group's fearless leader and an incredible role model for anyone who wants to make the world a better place.

ANNIE HAS A graduate degree in city and regional planning. She has also helped advise companies (including Ben and Jerry's—ice cream, yum) on how to lower their eco-impact.

OVER THE COURSE of her career, Annie has traveled to more than forty countries to study both factories and trash dumps.

ACT LIKE ANNIE

This one is super-easy: buy less stuff! The next time you want something trendy—cool jeans, the latest phone, a new toy—consider where it comes from and where it will go when you throw it out. If you really need it, can you buy it used or vintage?

MARGARET "MARDY" MURIE

B. 1902–D. 2003

Conservationist & Wilderness Champion

When you roam and explore rural Alaska as a kid, you're pretty much guaranteed to adore and feel at home in nature. Margaret Murie, whose nickname was Mardy, certainly did. She spent part of her childhood in Fairbanks, Alaska. Her love of the outdoors motivated her to conserve and protect wilderness from being destroyed when she grew up.

Back in the 1920s, when sexism was even worse than it is today, not a lot of women went to college. Mardy was the first woman to graduate from the University of Alaska—an early sign of what a pioneer she was. Her trailblazing lifestyle continued after graduation. She married Olaus Murie, a biologist for the US Fish and Wildlife Service, a government agency dedicated to protecting both. They loved nature adventures so much that their 1924 wedding was a sunrise ceremony by the Yukon River at 3 a.m.! Can you imagine what kind of a party that must have been?

Mardy got deeply involved with her husband's work, including when he spent seventeen years as the president of the Wilderness Society, an organization that protects wild places. Their life always involved outdoor expeditions. They even spent their honeymoon researching caribou (which are the reindeer of North America) and traveling by boat and dogsled!

When the Muries moved from Alaska to Wyoming, where Olaus studied elk—tracking and counting them—Mardy and their kids joined him camping and backpacking wherever he roamed. Although the Muries never lived in Alaska full time after moving to Wyoming, they returned for visits. On one trip back, they came up with a plan to get the government to create an Alaskan wildlife refuge, which would protect wild animals and the land. It was a long battle involving many other people, but it eventually worked. In 1960, President Dwight D. Eisenhower created the Arctic National Wildlife Refuge, with more than 8 million acres. President Carter increased this to more than 19 million acres in 1980! These preserved acres protect untold amounts of wildlife and resources—an amazing accomplishment.

To conserve even more wilderness, the Muries pushed Congress to pass the Wilderness Act, which would protect land all across the United States from development. Unfortunately,

Olaus died shortly before the Wilderness Act became law, but Mardy was at the White House to witness the act being signed in 1964. It has been called the most important environmental protection legislation in the history of the United States. She continued their conservation activism after Olaus's death for many years.

The Muries' Wyoming ranch was designated a National Historic District in 1997. Today it's called the Murie Center and is used for conservation education. Murie wrote several books about nature, the most well known of which is *Two in the Far North*. It's still available at your local library today. Check it out! In the book, Mardy wrote, "Do I dare to believe that one of my great-grandchildren may someday journey to the Sheenjek and still find the gray wolf trotting across the ice of Lobo Lake?" Her work protecting land for all Americans made this scenario—and many others—possible for many more children than just her great-grandchildren. What a legacy!

MARDY, OFTEN CALLED the grandmother of the conservation movement, lived to be 101 years old.

MARDY GOT MANY honors for her inspiring work, including an Audubon Medal in 1980 and a John Muir Award in 1983 from Sierra Club, an important environmental organization. In 1998, President Bill Clinton awarded her the Presidential Medal of Freedom—the most prestigious award an American who doesn't work for the US government can get.

ACT LIKE MARDY

Go on an adventure and get inspired! Head to the woods or your state park and go camping, canoeing, and hiking. Always protect the land around you. Join forces with environmental organizations protecting wildlife and nature near where you live.

PEGGY SHEPARD

B. 1946

Environmental Justice Advocate & Community Builder

Community, not the environment, was the main focus of Peggy Shepard's childhood. Her father was the only Black doctor delivering babies in their small New Jersey town, and young Peggy made house calls all over with him. She also grew up watching her mom volunteer with many local organizations. By nine, Peggy was already building community, launching her own groups and clubs! In college, she studied English and then worked in publishing—she was the first Black reporter for the *Indianapolis News*. The environment became her focus only after she was elected Democratic district leader in northern New York City and she learned that environmental issues were making her community sick.

It used to be that when you flushed your toilet in New York City, it went pretty much straight into the Hudson River! Not surprisingly, the Hudson became unswimmable, and the fish in it died. It really needed to be cleaned, so a sewage treatment plant was opened in West Harlem, Peggy's community. Unfortunately, the plant polluted the air and made people ill. The sewage plant in West Harlem was originally supposed to be built in a white, upper-middle-class neighborhood but was moved. Environmentally harmful things like sewage plants are usually built in neighborhoods where low-income people, and often people of color, live. This is called "environmental racism." Who wants a sewage plant in their backyard? No one! Peggy fought against this sewage plant for many years. Eventually, in 1988, a lawsuit against New York City resulted in a $1.1 million settlement and a $55 million commitment to upgrade the sewage facility to stop its pollution.

Peggy's work was just beginning—the sewage plant was only one of her community's environmental problems. She cofounded an organization, West Harlem Environmental Action (WE ACT) for Environmental Justice, to help. One of WE ACT's big projects over the past two decades has been getting the city to clean up the bus emissions as well as bus depots polluting West Harlem's air. Progress can take a long time.

It's just not fair that the bulk of a city's pollution should be dumped in any one community. Everyone has an equal right to a clean and a healthy environment. That's why WE ACT works on a range of environmental health and justice issues. Environmental justice is the antidote to

29

environmental racism. WE ACT partners with a local hospital to study the health of Harlem community members. The organization also works for safer housing, free of things like lead (which harms developing brains) and mold (which causes allergies). It's also addressing how the climate crisis impacts the community.

Environment doesn't just mean nature. It's your immediate environment, too: your house, your school, and your playground. All of these should be safe. A community doesn't need to be wealthy to demand this safety, but it does need to be organized. Peggy has combined her deep knowledge of how community works with social activism. Her expert organizing around environmental hazards has helped one traditionally low-income urban neighborhood in particular, but it has also led to national and even international change.

IN 1991, PEGGY was involved in creating the seventeen Principles of Environmental Justice at the First National People of Color Environmental Leadership Summit. These principles are now used by people all over the world. WE ACT is also the lead organizer of the Environmental Justice Leadership Forum on Climate Change, a coalition of organizations.

PEGGY WAS GIVEN an important Heinz Award for the Environment for "her courageous advocacy and determined leadership in combatting environmental injustice in urban America."

ACT LIKE PEGGY

Organize a classroom panel to discuss environmental issues affecting your community. Conduct a survey of your classmates' views on environmental issues and activities that they can do to address them. Talk to your parents about recycling and ways your family can help improve the environment.

CHARLES MOORE

B. 1947

Sea Captain & Plastic Pollution Explorer

If you know about the three Rs—reduce, reuse, recycle—then you already know we have a serious global plastic problem on our hands. We make way too much plastic—and even worse, we make it using fossil fuels, which are also bad for the environment—and we don't have strong enough systems in place to truly recycle the amount that we create. Some plastic, like a fork for takeout food, we use only for a few minutes and then throw out. And that fork will exist forever. What a waste! The result is tons of plastic in our environment, especially in our oceans. As Charles Moore has explained, "the ocean is downhill from everywhere," so a lot of our waste ends up in our precious oceans. Captain Charles would know: during a yachting competition across the Pacific Ocean in 1997, he discovered what's now called the Great Pacific Garbage Patch, a giant area of floating garbage twice the size of Texas.

Charles has described his discovery like this: "There were shampoo caps and soap bottles and plastic bags and fishing floats as far as I could see. Here I was in the middle of the ocean, and there was nowhere I could go to avoid the plastic." Now he works to raise awareness about and reduce plastic pollution through his organization, the Algalita Marine Research Foundation. As part of his work there, he also trains teachers, educates kids, and hosts a yearly youth summit. He believes young people are uniquely capable of making the changes the world needs.

Plastic floating in water isn't just bad because it's ugly when it washes up on beaches where people play and swim. Water is a system of life. Seabirds scavenge and eat the plastic—it looks like food to them—then feed it to their young. Chemicals in plastic aren't meant to be eaten and can lead to health problems for these species, including diseases. Marine animals like turtles can also get strangled by the plastic rings that hold together six-packs of soda cans. Bigger plastic pieces break down into tiny pellets, and seabirds as well as fish eat them. The bigger the fish, the more they eat, and potentially toxic plastic chemicals build up in their flesh. Some humans eat these fish—and therefore the plastic, too. Charles speaks often in public about plastic pollution. Once he said, "Only we humans make waste that nature can't digest."

One solution people have suggested is to gather all the garbage, cleaning our oceans of plastic. But this is too big and expensive a task. What we need to do is to stop plastic at the source. Charles isn't certain this is possible—after all, it seems everything is made of plastic these days. Companies that make plastic don't want to stop; plastic earns them money. But consumers—that's us!—can help by putting pressure on our governments and also the companies we buy products from. Let them know we don't want to be a throwaway society that continues to create and throw out single-use plastic packaging. We can also demand increased recycling. Charles says under 5 percent of plastics are actually recycled. That's way too low!

The next time you see plastic on a beach or on a hike, pick it up and do what it takes to recycle it. This may feel small in the face of a giant garbage patch, but every action counts and raises awareness.

DID YOU KNOW your water bottle in California may wind up as garbage all the way in the Philippines? Say no to single-use plastics!

CAPTAIN CHARLES HAS been back to the Great Plastic Garbage Patch to continue studying it since he first came across it. In 1999, his research discovered that the plastic there outweighed natural zooplankton (live organisms found in the water) six to one. That is not okay!

ACT LIKE CHARLES

Be real. Be brave. Be persistent. Investigate environmental hazards and speak out about them, no matter what people might think. Don't be afraid to look under a rock no one has ever picked up before.

PRECIOUS BRADY-DAVIS

B. 1985

Trans Activist & Environmentalist

Burning any fossil fuel, like oil to heat a house or gasoline to drive a car, releases pollution into the air and contributes to climate change. But coal-fired power plants, which make electricity, are considered extra-dirty—they release a bunch of poison into the air, like mercury and also carbon dioxide, which heats up the earth. That's why replacing coal with cleaner energy, including solar and wind, has a big and positive impact. Precious Brady-Davis's work at Sierra Club, an environmental organization that has been around for many decades, has focused on ways to move beyond coal as an energy source.

Precious is a transgender woman of color, and research has proven that the climate crisis harms women as well as people of color more than others. Communities of color are more affected by things like air pollution, more likely to live in places that flood, and have higher rates of environmentally linked diseases. Precious herself suffered from asthma and allergies growing up. So, her environmental work directly impacts her life. She is also deeply involved with LGBTQ (lesbian, gay, bisexual, transgender, queer) rights and racial equality.

Precious never expected to have an environmental job. After Donald Trump became president of the United States, she was upset—both by his efforts to roll back legal protections for transgender people and by his attempts to take apart crucial long-standing environmental laws. Trump even backed out of an important international climate pact—the Paris Climate Agreement. This is what inspired Precious to join Sierra Club's communications team.

Most of the scientists and activists doing environmental work today, especially the ones who get interviewed by the media, are white men. Being a biracial trans woman environmentalist means Precious has a unique opportunity to reach out to and involve communities that sometimes feel excluded by the environmental movement. Precious knows that people fighting for LGBTQ rights or racial justice might not also be working to protect the earth, and vice versa. She wants to be the bridge between these important groups, to help people

understand that climate justice and racial justice are part of the same fight. Precious believes these movements overlap and can learn from each other.

On an episode of the Sierra Club podcast series *The Land I Trust,* Precious said her personal history informs her environmental work: "Anywhere I go, I change the culture. I leave the place better than I found it, and I think that's how we should treat the environment." The environmental movement is lucky to have her!

···

THINGS HAVE A way of coming full circle: Precious actually interned for Sierra Club while growing up in Nebraska.

PRECIOUS HAS GREAT memories of playing outdoors as a kid. These days, she's more likely to be photographed in a dress than the environmentalist's uniform of hiking gear. But she's proving environmentalists can wear—and be—anything. It's a movement with room for everyone!

ACT LIKE PRECIOUS

···

Be yourself. Get involved in all of your communities. Environmentalism, racial rights, and gender rights are all connected. It's all public health.

SARAH TOUMI

B. 1987

Tree Planter & Sustainable Agriculture Entrepreneur

Sarah Toumi was born in France to a French mother and a Tunisian father. When she was nine, she traveled to Tunisia, a country in North Africa, for the first time. Even at a young age, Sarah got involved in working on social causes there, enlisting her father to help. They built youth centers and libraries and also worked to empower women, who traditionally did not have many rights in her dad's home country.

In 2011, there was a revolution in Tunisia, which brought in a new government and a promise of change. So Sarah returned to Tunisia. There, she saw how the climate crisis was already harming the Tunisian people. Because the weather was getting hotter and drier, Tunisia's desert was growing bigger—a process called desertification. Through soil erosion and lack of rain, the desert sand was literally taking over the villages, especially rural ones. Desertification is like something out of a horror movie! Sarah learned that 75 percent of Tunisia's land was becoming desert. This was incredibly bad news for the farmers, who need to work the land to earn money. Not a lot can grow in sand.

Sarah went to rural villages and asked local women whether they were being impacted by the desertification. They answered yes. So, in 2012, Sarah founded Acacias for All, a project to keep the sand from taking over, help the farmers, and fight poverty at the same time. Her idea was to get local people to plant trees, which would stop the erosion and therefore the sand. The trees would also create job opportunities and help with pollution, because they act as air filters.

She began by training women to plant one thousand acacia trees. Sarah researched and chose acacias because they grow well even in dry desert environments without a lot of water or harmful chemical fertilizers. Also, acacia trees can be used to make commercial products—Arabic gum and moringa oil—that out-of-work farmers who had been impacted by the desertification could harvest and sell for money. Arabic gum is used as an ingredient in food products, while moringa oil can be found in cosmetics like moisturizing face creams, natural makeup, and hair conditioner.

Sarah's vision worked! The trees grew, and their roots did help reduce erosion and decrease desertification. The trees also gave new life to the soil. In this richer soil, farmers

39

in many villages were able to plant crops other than acacia trees. These were plants that also grow well in the area's dry and hot climate, don't require a lot of water, and can be sold to make money. So the simple act of planting a tree reestablished what's called **biodiversity**—a variety of plants—there. Sarah also organized the farmers to work together to sell what they grow.

Acacias for All's sustainable farming methods have now expanded outside Tunisia to villages in neighboring countries, including Algeria and Morocco. Planting trees in all these locations fights desertification and reduces greenhouse gas emissions. The trees also give farmers as well as local youth hope and a purpose—growing and selling natural local products. This is so inspiring—join forces with Sarah and plant a tree today!

IN 2013, THE French government named Acacias for All as one of the one hundred innovations poised to shape the future of sustainable development in all of Africa.

SINCE ACACIAS FOR All launched in 2012, the organization has planted at least 650,000 trees—and counting!

ACT LIKE SARAH

Think of a simple solution to help the planet and people alike, then work with others to make it happen on a bigger and bigger scale. Starting now!

ALEXANDRIA VILLASEÑOR

B. 2005

Climate Activist & Student

Reading about the climate crisis is one thing, but experiencing it personally is another. When one of the worst wildfires in California history burned in November 2018, Alexandria Villaseñor and her family had to stuff wet towels under doors to keep smoke from getting into a house where they were visiting relatives. Even though Alexandria was staying several hours away from the climate crisis–linked fire, the smoke was still so bad that it triggered her asthma. To protect her health and escape the smoke, Alexandria went home to New York. It took her weeks to feel better. When she finally did, one thing was clear: she wanted to join the climate fight.

Alexandria didn't know how to get involved until she saw the Swedish teenage activist Greta Thunberg speak at a climate conference. She learned about Greta's weekly Fridays for Future climate strikes outside the Swedish Parliament, where she protested to raise awareness instead of going to school. Inspired, Alexandria started her own strikes outside the United Nations in New York City. For many weeks and in all kinds of weather, Alexandria climate-striked alone. But the Fridays for Future movement was taking off globally, and she wasn't alone for long. Less than one year after her first Friday strike, Alexandria was speaking in front of a crowd of 250,000 climate strikers! Some activists in that crowd, including Greta herself, were in New York City for the 2019 UN Climate Action Summit. To help motivate and organize other youth activists, Alexandria started her own group, called Earth Uprising. She refers to it as a battle cry, not an organization.

Before the California wildfires inflamed her asthma and then her activism, Alexandria was just like any other kid you know. She played with her friends and had hobbies. These days, her peers are other global youth climate activists, and they're in close contact thanks to social media. These kids are doing the very adult work of fighting for our future and demanding the right to a safe and stable planet. They want an end to fossil fuels. They want clean energy. They want the governments and corporations responsible for heating up the earth to listen to the scientific facts about the climate and make big changes. Alexandria is also trying

to fix the lack of climate education in the United States by sharing science and facts with other students.

Alexandria has expressed frustration that by the time she's old enough to vote, it will be too late to act on climate. The urgent time for action is now. But today's voters and the politicians they elect are moving too slowly toward solutions. You might think that one kid striking alone with a sign can't make a difference, but Alexandria is proof that's not true! World leaders are noticing. It's not up to children to save the world—or even fair that they should have to try—but it's a good thing for all of us that Alexandria and her fellow international climate strikers are taking a stand. If more of us can be as loud as she is, we'll have a better chance of winning this battle. Join her!

· ·

ALEXANDRIA AND A group of other youth activists (including Greta Thunberg) filed a complaint at the United Nations stating that the world—and five polluting countries in particular—is violating their rights as children according to the UN Convention on the Rights of the Child.

PARENTS AREN'T USUALLY happy when their kids skip school, but for something as important as climate striking, they might feel differently! Alexandria's parents are supportive of her activism and are often seen with her at public events. She said they even let her pick who they voted for in the 2020 presidential election.

ACT LIKE ALEXANDRIA
· ·
Even if you're too young to vote, you can still make signs, attend protests, and make your battle cry heard—loud and clear.

RACHEL CARSON   B. 1907–D. 1964

Ecologist & Author

In 1962, Rachel Carson published an important book called *Silent Spring*. It was full of new information about the link between human-made chemicals and the health of our planet. Sometimes books written by scientists can be hard to read (or even a little boring . . .), but Rachel, a beautiful writer, was great at explaining confusing scientific research in a simple way that made people want to read about it. The book got so many people concerned, it launched America's modern environmental movement.

In *Silent Spring*, Rachel explained how the pesticides people use to kill insects and plants actually reach far beyond their target—and destroy our environment. It's obvious if you think about it. When someone sprays a pesticide to get rid of ants or mosquitoes the chemical doesn't stop working after it kills the specific bugs it was meant for. After it zaps the insects, it continues to harm everything else it comes into contact with: farmland, soil, waterways, wild animals—and even people.

Pesticides and other chemicals (which Rachel called "biocides") get into the human body after they contaminate our food and drinking water. Humans are part of the natural world, just like frogs, birds, bees, and fish. Rachel wrote, "These sprays, dusts and aerosols are now applied almost universally to farms, gardens, forests and homes—nonselective chemicals that have the power to kill every insect, the good and the bad. Can anyone believe it is possible to lay down such a barrage of poisons on the surface of the earth without making it unfit for all life?"

Even as a young kid growing up exploring nature in rural Pennsylvania, Rachel wanted to be a writer and was interested in science. She studied at a marine biology lab and then got a degree in zoology from Johns Hopkins University. This was back in 1932 when women scientists were pretty rare! Rachel figured out how to blend science with her love of writing at a few jobs, including as editor of scientific publications for the US Fish and Wildlife Service.

When *Silent Spring* was published, big companies that made pesticides tried to claim Rachel's research wasn't good. In fact, it was so good that it inspired the US president, John F. Kennedy, to have the President's Science Advisory Committee look into the dangers of biocides! Rachel also testified before Congress in 1963.

Silent Spring wasn't Rachel's first book, but sadly it was her last; she died of breast cancer at age fifty-six, two years after *Silent Spring* came out and before she got to see what an incredible impact her work would have. In 1970, the United States launched the Environmental Protection Agency (EPA), thanks, in part, to Rachel's work. And DDT, a dangerous pesticide that she wrote about in *Silent Spring,* was banned in 1972.

Many dangerous pesticides are still available for anyone to buy. It's a shame that years after Rachel told the world how dangerous they are, untested harmful chemicals are still being sold to farmers and to people for use at home. Many modern scientists continue Rachel's research on chemicals still harming birds, bees, wildlife, and humans. Each time one gets banned or a government requires better chemical regulations, that's thanks to Rachel Carson!

SIXTEEN YEARS AFTER her death, in 1980, Rachel Carson was awarded the US Presidential Medal of Freedom by President Jimmy Carter.

SILENT SPRING WAS her most famous book, but Rachel wrote three others that are also well worth reading: *Under the Sea-Wind* (1941), *The Sea Around Us* (1951), and *The Edge of the Sea* (1955).

ACT LIKE RACHEL

Avoid synthetic pesticides, insecticides, and herbicides wherever you can! Eat **organic** food, which is grown without them. Don't use biocides on your own plants, garden, or in your home. If your school uses harmful sprays for pests or weeds on its lawn, start a community petition asking to switch to safer products.

EUNICE NEWTON FOOTE

B. 1819–D. 1888

Climate Science Pioneer & Women's Rights Activist

Back in the 1850s, female scientists were rare. Science was a man's world. This is a big reason you may not have heard of amateur scientist Eunice Newton Foote before. But she was a real force! As a kid, her parents sent her to one of the few American schools at the time that even taught girls science. Good thing they did, because the research she went on to do on carbon dioxide (CO_2) and climate warming was groundbreaking.

Her experiments were simple. Basically, she filled glass containers with various gases and placed them in the sunlight. Then she measured their temperatures. Foote discovered that the one containing CO_2 trapped more heat and stayed hot for a long time. She formed a theory that what happened in this jar could apply to the planet, too: trapped CO_2 in the atmosphere could have changed the temperature in past eras. It's pretty basic science without a lot of data, but linking CO_2 to global warming was at that point a completely new idea. Later, male scientists ran more complicated experiments and got comparable results.

"An atmosphere of that gas would give to our earth a high temperature; and if as some suppose, at one period of its history the air had mixed with it a larger proportion than at present, an increased temperature . . . must have necessarily resulted," Eunice wrote. Her paper about her experiments, called "Circumstances Affecting the Heat of Sun's Rays," was presented—by a male colleague—at an 1856 meeting of the American Association for the Advancement of Science.

A few years later, an Irish physicist named John Tyndall did similar research. As a man, John had more training and resources than Eunice. Although John came to basically the same conclusions, Eunice's research—a discovery that became the foundation of climate science—was never formally published. She never got the credit she deserved. Until recently.

In 2010, a retired geologist named Raymond Sorenson came across Eunice's research and wrote a paper about her, "Eunice Foote's Pioneering Research on CO_2 and Climate Warming." In it, he explained how Eunice's experiments showed what we now call the **"greenhouse effect."** Raymond concluded that Eunice "deserves credit for being an innovator on the topic

47

of CO_2 and its potential impact on global climate warming." It's wild to consider how many other women have advanced science without ever being recognized for their important contributions. Better late than never!

. . . .

EUNICE FOOTE IS one of the people who signed the 1848 Seneca Falls Declaration, the manifesto made during the first women's rights convention in the United States that stated women should be allowed to vote in elections. Her signature is right under well-known suffragist Elizabeth Cady Stanton's. Eunice's husband, Elisha, signed, too.

ELISHA FOOTE, EUNICE'S husband, was a judge and the head of the US Patent Office. Their daughter, Mary, married senator John B. Henderson, one of the co-authors of the Thirteenth Amendment to the US Constitution, which banned slavery.

ACT LIKE EUNICE
. . . .

Be curious. Experiment. Study science and follow your interests. You never know what you might discover that could change the world.

JAMES HANSEN B. 1941

Climate Scientist & Truth Teller

The current climate crisis could have been stopped, or at least slowed, if we had listened to James Hansen more than thirty years ago. He researched greenhouse gases at the National Aeronautics and Space Administration (NASA). In 1981, he and some other scientists published an article in a journal called _Science_ showing that greenhouse gases, which trap heat in the atmosphere, had been increasing because of humans burning fossil fuels as well as other activities and would warm the earth in the years to come. A steadily warming earth would result in drought, melting ice sheets, and rising sea level in the twenty-first century. These alarming facts made the front page of the _New York Times_ with the headline: "Study Finds Warming Trend That Could Raise Sea Levels."

James was asked to testify before the US government in 1988. He described how global warming increases weather extremes. "It is time to stop waffling so much," he famously told a congressional committee, "and say that the evidence is pretty strong that the greenhouse effect is here." Speaking honestly about his research, James heroically risked his reputation and his job. Unfortunately, no one wanted to hear such scary news or to act on this incredibly important information, even though we already had available solutions to reduce greenhouse gas emissions. Instead, the world basically ignored James and continued to use fossil fuels greedily and carelessly.

Now, more than three decades since James testified in front of Congress, it's crystal clear he was right. Emissions have skyrocketed, and our planet is warmer than ever. Ocean temperatures are up, and we have experienced severe heat waves, melting glaciers, sea level rising, and more. Since the 1980s, James has avoided public speaking, focusing instead on research. In 2004, he decided to sound the alarm again. He wanted his grandchildren to know he did everything he could to warn the world to protect everyone's future. After he gave a few speeches, the White House told him he couldn't do more without NASA's approval. James told the media about this censorship, and the government backed off.

James has compared the climate crisis to a giant asteroid on a direct collision course with earth—with no one trying to divert the asteroid. The longer we wait, the more expensive it

51

will be to fix. And at some point soon we won't be able to fix it at all. Today, he's still urgently educating the world about the need to reduce greenhouse gases or risk everything from food shortages to mass extinction.

If the United States had done something about what James was saying back in 1988, the world would be very different today. Now is the time to finally listen: the science is clear, and we have the solutions for a clean energy future. James Hansen has been one of the earliest, loudest, and most consistent voices in the scientific community to warn us about climate change, and he wants all citizens of the world to help spread his urgent message. As he has said, we owe it to our children and our grandchildren.

JAMES HAS ADDED a few jobs to his resume over the years: film advisor and professor. He was Vice President Al Gore's science advisor on his 2006 documentary, *An Inconvenient Truth*. After leaving his job as director of the NASA Goddard Institute for Space Studies in 2013, he became an adjunct professor at Columbia University's Earth Institute.

JAMES'S GRANDDAUGHTER, SOPHIE Kivlehan, is one of twenty-one youth activists (including Xiuhtezcatl Martinez) who sued the US government for failing to protect the atmosphere for future generations. James acted as an expert witness for the case. A dedicated grandfather, he also wrote a 2009 book called *Storms of My Grandchildren: The Truth About the Coming Climate Catastrophe and Our Last Chance to Save Humanity*.

ACT LIKE JAMES

Speak honestly and loudly about climate change, even if what you're saying is unpopular. The science is clear, and the truth could not be more important.

OPHA PAULINE DUBE

B. 1960

Professor & IPCC Author

If you're curious about our changing climate, maybe you've watched YouTube videos of Greta Thunberg and heard her mention an "IPCC" report on the impacts of global warming. Here's what that means: IPCC stands for Intergovernmental Panel on Climate Change. The panel was founded by the United Nations in 1988 to review all the current science available about climate change and write it up in reports. These reports are an important tool used by the people in governments who make environmental policy—the rules about conserving natural resources and protecting the land, air, and water from pollution.

The scientists who are asked to be part of the IPCC are among the world's best. In 2018, when the IPCC released a special report on the impacts of 1.5 degrees Celsius of global warming, the panel was made up of eighty-six authors and review editors from thirty-nine countries. Opha Pauline Dube, who is from Botswana, in southern Africa, is one of the chosen eighty-six. She's an environmental change scientist. She goes by Pauline, and her official title is coordinating lead author of the Intergovernmental Panel on Climate Change. In 2007, the IPCC, including Pauline, shared the prestigious Nobel Peace Prize with US vice president Al Gore (see page 77) for their efforts to educate people about human-made climate change and to give the world the information needed to fight it. The IPCC is doing incredibly important work.

Pauline probably knows as much as anyone about climate science. She would wow you if she came over for dinner and told you all she has learned about droughts, what the world would look like if it warms up by 2 degrees Celsius, and the unique needs of the world's poorest countries. What's even more amazing than how much she knows is how much she *does*. Outside of her work with the IPCC, Pauline has taught both college and graduate students as an associate professor in the Department of Environmental Science at the University of Botswana. She's also co–editor in chief of an important scientific publication called *Current Opinion in Environmental Sustainability*. And she's involved with many committees in Botswana, including the Botswana Global Environmental Change Committee, which

she founded, and the Botswana Government National Climate Change Committee. She is a serious earth champion!

Pauline says climate work is her passion, and she's devoted to teaching other people what she knows. The IPCC reports are pretty long and dense for the average person to read and understand. They're really meant to provide up-to-date scientific information for the leaders who currently have the most power to make environmental laws and regulations. Still, the reports have strongly influenced the global conversation on urgent actions needed— from those policy makers, to youth climate activists, and all the way down to you.

SOME OF PAULINE'S specific climate-related work in Africa focuses on wildfires and drought. Rain has been decreasing in Africa. "Water is life," she has said. "With no water, Africa will be a dead continent." Less rain affects the amount of food that can be grown. It can also lead to the spread of diseases and energy shortages.

IF YOU WANT to be on the IPCC when you grow up, you need to study science. Pauline has a PhD in geographical science from the University of Queensland in Australia.

ACT LIKE PAULINE

Scientists matter. But even if science isn't your passion, you can follow your interests, learn about topics that you feel strongly about, and use your knowledge to make the world a better place.

DR. PHILIP LANDRIGAN

B. 1942

Pediatrician & Environmental Health Advocate

Phil Landrigan is known worldwide for his work on how toxic chemicals in the environment impact children's health. In the early 1970s, while working at the US Centers for Disease Control and Prevention (CDC), he studied children in Texas who lived near a lead ore smelter—a factory where rock is heated to separate out the lead in it. Unfortunately, lead, a naturally occurring heavy metal, causes brain damage in children—exposure to it can make you less smart, shorten your attention span, and result in trouble controlling impulsive behavior. Scientists thought only large amounts of lead caused brain damage, but Phil found that even low levels can harm kids. Thanks to his research, the Environmental Protection Agency wound up removing lead from gasoline and paint. This resulted in a 95 percent decline in the United States of kids with lead poisoning as well as a reduction in criminal activity. That's pretty amazing! Other countries followed the United States' example. Phil said this makes him feel good.

Growing up in Boston, Phil played in the woods as a Boy Scout. He was inspired to go to medical school by two doctors: his uncle plus his family doctor. After graduating from Boston College in 1963, he attended Harvard Medical School. Working in public health was somewhat accidental. At that time, people were being drafted for the Vietnam War, and he was sent by the US Public Health Service to work at the CDC, where he spent fifteen years. In 1985, he began working as a member of the faculty at Mount Sinai School of Medicine in New York, where he also became director of its Center for Children's Health and the Environment. In 2018, at an age when most people retire, Phil headed home to become director of Boston College's Global Public Health initiative—researching the impacts of environmental pollution.

Throughout his career, Phil's focus has been on how children are uniquely vulnerable to harm from chemicals. In the United States, chemical safety laws are weak. New chemicals don't need to be tested for safety before they're used in everyday products—from our bubble bath to our toys. This doesn't make sense. Since Phil first researched lead, there has been a huge increase in the number of human-made chemicals kids are exposed to daily— even before they are born, in their mother's wombs. These chemicals are found in plastics (food packaging, sippy cups), cosmetics (diaper cream, shampoo), electronics (tablets, computers), and even our food, from pesticides that are sprayed on crops. Different chemicals have different health impacts, and because humans are exposed to so many, it's sometimes unclear which, exactly, are making people sick. It is clear that childhood diseases are on the rise: learning disabilities, autism, obesity, asthma, and cancer rates are all up.

By connecting the dots between our environment and the health of kids, Phil has brought about so much positive change. American kids have actually gotten smarter! He was involved with a report on pesticides and children's health that influenced the US Food Quality Protection Act of 1996. He worked on setting up the EPA's Office of Children's Health Protection. Phil's reach has been global, too; he has consulted with the World Health Organization. And his research has educated many families on how to protect their children from toxic chemicals at home—maybe even yours.

PHIL HAS WON lots of awards for his work, including the EPA Environmental Health Champion Award, the Medal for Lifetime Achievement in Public Health from New York Academy of Medicine, the Meritorious Service Medal of the US Public Health Service, and the Lifetime Achievement Award from the Children's Health Environmental Coalition.

THIS DOCTOR LIKES to write! He has written more than five hundred scientific papers and five books, including *Children and Environmental Toxins: What Everyone Needs to Know*, cowritten with his wife, Mary. They met at college, where she was studying chemistry.

ACT LIKE PHIL

To make a difference cleaning up the environment, you don't have to be a doctor. But these are not easy problems, so to solve them you need an education. Go to school and get the appropriate training in public health, environmental science, or medicine. You also need to have a moral compass. There are people with environmental science training who work for the gas and oil industry. Your ethical focus should be on improving people's lives.

THE TRIMATES
DIAN FOSSEY
JANE GOODALL
BIRUTÉ GALDIKAS

B. 1932–D. 1985

B. 1934

B. 1946

Primatologists & Conservationists

These three amazing women have something in common: studying primates. Jane Goodall, from England, observes chimpanzees in Tanzania; Dian Fossey, from America, worked with gorillas in Congo and then Rwanda; and Biruté Galdikas, a Lithuanian Canadian, focuses on the orangutans in Indonesian Borneo. What's your favorite primate? The Trimates got their nickname (which is a blend of the prefix "tri," which means "three," and the word "primates"), from the well-known paleoanthropologist and archaeologist Louis Leakey. Louis was a mentor to all three women, and he helped them find the money they needed for their research, beginning with Jane in 1960.

Although they weren't the first scientists to visit remote locations to study animals in person, the Trimates, starting with Jane, took a totally different approach. Instead of briefly visiting and doing most of their research from afar in a laboratory, they actually lived among their primates in their natural habitats for many years. This gave them all a unique opportunity to learn everything about their subjects—especially the complex ways they interact socially, including in family life. Observing primates, human beings' closest biological relatives, is important scientific work; the Trimates' findings have helped the world understand so much about human behavior.

Studying animals in their natural habitat can be tricky and expensive, and it requires cooperation from local governments and people who live nearby. The locations are often hard to reach, and there are certainly no hotels or restaurants in such remote places! More seriously, there are political concerns, including dealing with elected officials who don't want researchers poking around. Dian even had to relocate from Congo to Rwanda after a rebellion in 1967.

As they observed primates in the wild, the Trimates also witnessed many environmental problems. This motivated them all to become conservationists, working to preserve the natural

habitats of their beloved subjects. Biruté has seen the destruction of tropical rain forests, and her orangutans have become endangered. Jane has recorded population decline, increased mining, illegal hunting, and the illegal capturing (or poaching) of wild animals. Dian grew so vocally opposed to both eco-unfriendly wildlife tourism and poaching that people say it's why she was eventually murdered in 1985—to stop her from speaking out.

The Trimates went on three brave and separate journeys, changed science, made history, and have inspired other scientists to enter the world's most remote locations to study and hopefully save our vanishing species and changing earth. Although their original intention was to document primate behavior, their overall work has morphed into one of the loudest calls to action to the world today. Their research institutes and foundations support this work as well as help spread information about primates. There's the Jane Goodall Institute, Dian's Karisoke Research Center, and Biruté's Orangutan Foundation International. We must do all we can to follow their lead and protect our many species and our shared environment at this moment of climate crisis and mass extinction.

THE TRIMATES WERE all inspired as children to work with animals. Jane always loved animals. Her father even gave her a chimp stuffed animal named after one born at the London Zoo. As a young woman, she traveled to Africa specifically to see animals in the wild, not in zoos. Dian's first love was the horses she rode starting at age six, while Biruté, who wanted to be an explorer growing up, was a big fan of Curious George as a kid.

WHEN JANE STARTED observing chimps, she didn't even have a college degree! But her work was so important that she was able to earn a PhD in ethology (the study of animal behavior) from Cambridge University in 1965. She's one of a very small group of people who have ever gotten a graduate degree from Cambridge without having an undergraduate degree first.

ACT LIKE THE TRIMATES

Follow your dreams. Be observant. And always protect natural habitat for wildlife and humans alike.

SANDRA STEINGRABER B. 1959

Ecologist & Activist

Pollutants in the environment—our air, water, and soil—don't stay put. They ripple out and touch all living beings on earth, including humans. Sandra Steingraber, a scientist, teacher, and writer, studies how the environment affects human health. She's one of today's fiercest fighters in the battle against toxic chemicals in our environment.

There are so many environmental pollutants today that even babies are being born polluted; scientists have found hundreds of chemicals in umbilical cord blood and in breast milk! These are everyday chemicals, things like pesticides sprayed on food crops, solvents for dry-cleaning clothes, and flame retardants used to protect household items like furniture and electronics in case of fire. You don't have to be a scientist to know that these chemicals shouldn't be in people's bodies, especially the delicate bodies of babies. Different chemicals have different effects, but being exposed to even small amounts of some of them as a baby can lead to health issues later in life: learning delays, asthma, cancer, and more.

Sandra grew up along the Illinois River in an area with a lot of manufacturing as well as farming. She was diagnosed with bladder cancer when she was only twenty years old, but she survived. Sandra's unique skill is translating confusing science about the environment and health into beautiful stories. In her 1997 book, *Living Downstream: An Ecologist's Personal Investigation of Cancer and the Environment,* she looks into the link between the cancer rates in the town she grew up in and environmental toxins. Steingraber also wrote *Having Faith: An Ecologist's Journey to Motherhood* and *Raising Elijah: Protecting Our Children in an Age of Environmental Crisis.* Faith and Elijah are her children's names.

Sandra has testified as an environmental health expert before government officials in Europe, as well as in the United States, where current chemical regulations are very weak. The United States has laws requiring that medicines be tested for human safety before they can be sold, but there are no similar requirements for industrial chemicals. More than 80,000 new chemicals have been introduced in the United States since World War II that have not been tested enough for how they might impact human health! The companies that make and sell these chemicals pressure the US government not to change the laws to protect people, since producing them earns them profits.

Today, Sandra's work on toxic chemicals has shifted to include fighting fracking, a destructive way of extracting natural gas from underground rock. Natural gas can be used for heating, among other things. Getting it out of the earth involves injecting poisonous chemicals, explosives, and a lot of water at very high pressure into the ground to break the rock and release the gas to be captured. Sandra's New York home sits above the specific kind of rock that contains natural gas and that energy companies want to frack. In 2012, she became a cofounder of the group New Yorkers Against Fracking. New York State decided to ban fracking in 2014, but fracking still happens elsewhere.

All of Sandra's work—as an author, a teacher, and a "fracktivist"—has a shared goal: to make pollution the problem of the industries and companies that create it, not the people who are harmed by it. In Sandra's environmental and human rights movement, being silent is as bad as agreeing with the polluters. It's a good thing—for all of us—that she's making so much noise.

IN 2011, SANDRA won the very important Heinz Award for her extraordinary service to the environment. It comes with a $100,000 prize, which she donated to the anti-fracking movement.

SANDRA HAS BEEN called the "new Rachel Carson." This is fitting because Sandra has said that Rachel Carson and her book *Silent Spring* were her call to arms.

ACT LIKE SANDRA

Get active and do your part, even if it's a small one. "We are all members of a great human orchestra," Sandra once said, "and it is now time to play the Save the World Symphony. You do not have to play a solo, but you do have to know what instrument you hold and find your place in the score."

WAN GANG

B. 1952

Electric Car Expert & Hydrogen Fuel Cell Enthusiast

We all know that the gasoline we use to power our cars is bad for our environment. And even though electric vehicles (EVs) that don't use gasoline exist, in almost every country—including many that are responsible for most of the world's pollution, like the United States—EVs just aren't that popular. Yes, a small number of people drive and love EVs, and some EV owners even get their electricity through solar and wind power so they can charge their electric car batteries with the cleanest energy available. But in most places, electric cars just haven't taken off—yet.

There's one exception: China. At the moment, EVs are more popular in China than anywhere else in the world. And one person deserves most of the credit for this: Wan Gang, the Chinese minister of science and technology. China has severe air pollution, and people there are on the lookout for ways to make it better. Wan promoted the environmental benefits of electric vehicles, won the Chinese government's support, and made EVs widespread in a pretty short time. This earned him a nickname: the "father of the electric car."

Wan has said we all have a shared responsibility to cope with climate change and to reduce emissions. That's why the EV father is constantly searching for the next big technology. Wan studied as a mechanical engineer and worked at Audi, a car company. He also held various other jobs including president of Tongji University in Shanghai, the biggest city in China. He's betting the next big thing will be hydrogen, which can be used to produce energy in a clean, nonpolluting way. That's why he's now trying to promote fuel cell vehicles (FCV), which are powered by hydrogen. The only thing FCVs emit into the air is water vapor. Talk about a cleaner technology! As vice chairman of China's national advisory body for policy making, Wan is setting up systems in a few regions to try hydrogen out. These trials are tests of how to produce, store, transport, and distribute hydrogen as a fuel, because these aspects of the process are a little challenging at the moment. If the tests go well, he would like to convert China to using mostly hydrogen-powered vehicles.

Hydrogen FCVs have actually been around for a while, but car shoppers don't choose them for a few reasons, including their high price tags. Still, hydrogen cars have advantages over electric ones. Refueling with hydrogen is much faster than charging an electric car, for

example. Depending on the type of charger you use and battery you have, charging an EV can take many hours, while FCVs take mere minutes—similar to the time it takes to fill up with gasoline. Hydrogen FCVs can also go farther than electric cars before needing to refuel. FCVs have a range of about three hundred miles, while most EVs currently for sale can't go farther than a hundred miles before recharging. This range has been expanding, though, as electric car technology develops.

China has very little oil of its own. That means the country has to import all the gasoline needed for use in traditional cars. This is part of the reason electric cars are so popular there—they don't require anything imported. Neither do hydrogen FCVs.

It would be a monumental positive change for the environment if all the cars in the world ran on electric batteries instead of gas, and hydrogen might be even better. That is Wan's dream. He has a great track record of making big automobile change in China so far. If he succeeds in setting up China as a hydrogen society, chances are you'll soon be seeing efficient and clean FCVs near where you live, too!

ACCORDING TO THE US Office of Energy Efficiency & Renewable Energy, hydrogen is the most abundant element on earth—that means there is plenty of it! It doesn't usually exist by itself in nature, so it gets produced from the compounds that contain it.

FUEL CELL SYSTEM cars are twice as efficient as gasoline system cars.

ACT LIKE WAN

Change is good and can even happen quickly under the right circumstances. Support new technologies that have the power to reduce emissions and save the earth!

CHRISTIANA FIGUERES   B. 1956

Former UN Climate Chief & Stubborn Optimist

For years, world leaders couldn't agree on how to stop climate change. Even though everyone knows drastic measures need to be taken, they have failed to come up with a global climate agreement—a way for nations to work together to make the changes we all need to save the planet. Most people didn't even think it was possible! Then Christiana Figueres showed up. She's a former Costa Rican diplomat who had been working on climate issues for many years. When she became executive secretary of the UN Framework Convention on Climate Change in 2010, things changed for the better. She worked her magic to persuade leaders to collaborate on the climate crisis and brought people together in a way no one else had before.

Thanks in part to Christiana, at the 2015 UN Climate Conference in Paris, France, 195 nations finally agreed to fight the climate crisis together! The Paris Agreement was a really big deal, and it was based on current climate science. International leaders agreed to take the steps needed to keep global warming below 2 degrees Celsius (or 3.6 degrees Fahrenheit) and to try not to go above 1.5 degrees Celsius (or 2.7 degrees Fahrenheit). Taking this action would protect the most vulnerable people on earth, improve all of our lives, and possibly slow down some of the effects of global warming.

Brokering a deal between so many people with different needs, opinions, cultures, and even languages was an amazing challenge. Christiana, who calls herself a "stubborn optimist," was well suited to the job because she knows how politicians think: her father was president of Costa Rica and her mother was an ambassador! She has also lived in many different countries—she attended college in America, got a graduate degree in anthropology in England, and has worked in Germany.

The changing environment has touched Christiana personally. The golden toad of the Costa Rican Monteverde cloud forest, which she remembers from her childhood, was one of the first species declared extinct because of climate change. This has fueled her mission to protect the planet. She's also motivated by her two children's futures. She believes today's adults are responsible for solving the climate crisis; it's not okay to hand this problem off to the next generation.

Since 2015, climate scientists have been warning the world about our warming planet with increasing urgency. Unfortunately, in 2017 there was a huge setback to the Paris Agreement when US president Donald Trump pulled out of the deal, which the previous president, Barack Obama, had signed. The science is clear that producing energy from fossil fuels like oil and coal is responsible for most of the greenhouse gases that are causing the climate crisis, and that renewable energy sources like wind and solar are the solution. Without the cooperation of the United States, one of the planet's biggest polluters, the Paris Agreement isn't the same. It won't be anywhere near as effective.

We can't afford to lose this climate battle. There is no other option. Christiana continues to focus on solutions: we can make more renewable energy, transportation can be cleaner, and food can be grown in a way that helps instead of harms the earth. Christiana is calling on every one of us to do our part—from global leaders to you and your family—to create a world where nature and humanity support each other. Who can say no to her?

CHRISTIANA HAS WON many awards for her climate work, from the French Legion of Honor to being inducted into the Earth Hall of Fame in Kyoto, Japan. *Fortune* magazine called her one of the World's 50 Greatest Leaders, and *Time* named her one of the One Hundred Most Influential Leaders in the World.

SCIENTISTS HAVE NAMED a newly discovered tropical moth, a wasp, and an orchid after Christiana! Costa Rica also created a postage stamp with her picture on it.

ACT LIKE CHRISTIANA

The climate crisis is urgent, so act now. Join climate protests whenever you can. If you can't vote yet, talk to your family about casting their votes for climate leaders. While you're at it, speak with them about switching to renewable energy sources, too.

ALEXANDRIA OCASIO-CORTEZ

B. 1989

Congresswoman & Green New Dealer

People can get stuck in a rut. We do the same things over and over again. Sometimes, it takes a newcomer to get things unstuck. When it comes to the US government and the climate crisis, Alexandria Ocasio-Cortez, also known as AOC, is that newcomer. At twenty-nine, she became the youngest US congresswoman in history, elected by New Yorkers in Queens and the Bronx where she grew up. AOC is considered a champion of working people. Along with being an environmentalist, she's also passionate about social and racial justice.

It makes no sense that important stuff like clean air and water are something politicians argue about. Everyone should want them! Unfortunately, some government officials prefer to protect polluters instead of defending the earth against pollution. Not AOC! Since arriving in Washington, DC, in 2019, she has teamed up with other politicians to create legislation like the Climate Equity Act and a resolution called the Green New Deal, which would get the US government to declare the climate crisis an emergency. The Green New Deal is a proposal—a ten-year plan for climate action. Its goal is to reduce emissions that are warming our planet, and it proposes methods like using cleaner energy sources, fixing transportation problems, building affordable housing, and creating "green jobs" so people can earn a living while helping the environment.

A few of the politicians supporting AOC and the Green New Deal ran for president in 2020. But some people don't like the Green New Deal, because they think it's trying to get too many things done at once. That's the point! Over the course of US history, in times of crisis, the government has introduced large projects designed to fix the huge problems of the day and to help its citizens. The Green New Deal is actually based on President Franklin Delano Roosevelt's 1930s New Deal, programs that were rolled out following the Great Depression. Sometimes you have to dream big and do a lot at once to make necessary changes.

AOC didn't grow up wanting to be a politician or an environmentalist. She studied economics and international relations at Boston University. While in college, her father died of

lung cancer. Her mom struggled to earn enough money to support the family by cleaning houses. After graduation, AOC wound up bartending and waitressing to help pay their bills. She has said these jobs trained her to listen well to people, an important part of being an elected official.

Even if the Green New Deal is never fully implemented, it's already been a success. It has moved the conversation about climate in America forward and helped make the climate crisis a major topic during the 2020 presidential election. The Green New Deal has also forced many elected officials to share their own plans for fighting the climate crisis with their constituencies. This all happened at the same time that President Trump was rolling back important environmental regulations put in place by President Obama and others who came before him. The Green New Deal has even influenced people outside the US government. It—and AOC—have inspired many to vote with the climate crisis in mind and to demand more from the politicians they elect. Young people have a big role to play in fixing the climate. AOC is an incredible new leader showing us the way forward.

AOC IS A member of another squad beyond the Earth Squad! The "Squad" is the nickname for four young Democratic congresswomen of color who were elected in 2018: AOC, Rashida Tlaib, Ayanna Pressley, and Ilhan Omar.

AOC'S FIRST POLITICAL job was as an intern for Senator Ted Kennedy during college. Before she became a congresswoman, she also volunteered for Senator Bernie Sanders's 2016 presidential campaign.

ACT LIKE ALEXANDRIA

Every generation needs a voice. AOC has become the voice for hers—maybe you will be the voice of yours. Jump in to make real change. Don't fear being disruptive or radical. You don't always have to play it safe to change the conversation, and you're never too young to make a difference.

INKA SAARA ARTTIJEFF

B. 1984

Reindeer Herder & Presidential Advisor

Most people agree that Santa lives at the North Pole. But if you talk to a Finnish person, they'll tell you he's specifically from Rovaniemi, a town in northern Finland. The Saami live there, too. They're the Indigenous people who were originally at the North Pole, way before this northern stretch of forest-filled land became part of Finland, Norway, Sweden, and Russia. Starting in the sixteenth century, outsiders began to take control of native Saami land and changed their way of living.

Inka Saara Arttijeff, the advisor to the president of the Saami Parliament in Finland, is a powerful voice for the environmental rights of Indigenous people, especially now at this moment of climate change. She grew up in a family of reindeer herders and has happy memories of the animals from her childhood. Reindeer herding is described in history books as a simple and respectful way of life. Traditionally, the Saami have relied on reindeer for food, clothing, and transportation. They also used reindeer to trade for other things they need, instead of using money. Reindeer migrate to find food depending on the season—from the forests in the winter to the coast in the summer.

Today, reindeer are being hurt by the climate crisis. Inka represents Finland at important international gatherings like the UN Climate Change Conference (COP), and she uses her love of reindeer to demonstrate to the world just how dire the climate situation is. Changing temperatures make it hard for the animals to graze. And because diseases and pests are usually kept at bay in freezing cold temperatures, the warmer weather in the region means both are able to spread more easily. As a result, herds are shrinking. Another environmental complication is that the forests where reindeer look for food are being cut down. Finland makes money by logging these forests and selling the wood. The Saami people are asking the Finnish government to stop clearing trees out of forests on their native land.

Climate change is also affecting other traditional Saami ways of living and earning money from nature, including fishing, making crafts from natural items, and hunting. Indigenous people all around the world are struggling with similar loss of their habitat and land, of their traditions, and even of their languages. Through her important work with Finland's Saami Parliament, Inka is working to protect a lot more than reindeer, too.

··

BECAUSE FINLAND IS so far north, the sun sets around 3 p.m. during the winter and doesn't rise until late morning. Finnish people are used to spending much of the season in total darkness. All the way up north, close to the Arctic Circle, it can stay dark twenty-four hours a day for part of the winter! The Finns make up for this during summer, when the sun never sets fully and they spend the season bathed in light.

INKA IS OFTEN photographed wearing traditional Saami clothing—shawls and intricate jewelry—and standing next to the president of the Finnish Saami Parliament, who wears similar clothes, including beautiful hats.

ACT LIKE INKA

··

Learn about and protect your family traditions, especially when they're being harmed by the climate crisis. You'll be helping to save the world while you're at it.

AL GORE

Climate Warrior & Vice President of the United States

Most people would say Al Gore is best known for being the forty-fifth vice president of the United States. He served two terms (that's eight years), starting in 1993, with President Bill Clinton. Before he was vice president, he was a longtime politician—beginning in 1976 as a Democratic congressman and later as a senator of his home state of Tennessee. Al Gore also ran for president two times, although he was unsuccessful. In 2000, he actually got the most votes (he won the "popular vote"), but he ultimately lost to President George W. Bush. Had he won, we would surely have stronger environmental laws and global agreements today.

That's because Al Gore's life's work is the environment. For decades, he has been using his position as a famous politician to let the world know about the dangers posed by global climate change—and about what solutions are available. Before he became a congressman, Vice President Gore's first job was as a reporter. Maybe his newspaper days are what make him so committed to spreading the truth far and wide.

Way back in 1981, Vice President Gore organized a congressional hearing on human-made global warming. He hasn't always succeeded in his efforts, but he has never stopped trying to warn people about the latest environmental science. He has worked directly with scientists, which is not true of many politicians. He even enlisted NASA to look for changes to our planet from space! He has also pushed for climate education. If you have studied global warming in school, it could be thanks to him.

Vice President Gore often represented the United States at global climate conferences. In 1992, he was the head of the US Senate delegation at the UN Conference on Environment and Development, which is where a treaty called the UN Framework Convention on Climate Change was signed by many countries. As vice president, he also helped broker a critical international climate agreement called the Kyoto Protocol, which called for reducing greenhouse gas emissions. There's an important UN Climate Change Conference that takes place every year at locations all around the world. Al Gore still attends this conference, COP, even though he's no longer a government official.

Since he left politics, Al Gore has focused even more on the climate crisis. In 2005, he founded The Climate Reality Project, an organization that trains people on how to talk about the climate crisis and its solutions. Gore's documentary about climate, *An Inconvenient Truth,* won two Oscars in 2006! In 2017, he made a follow-up documentary, *An Inconvenient Sequel: Truth to Power.* In the film, there are scenes of Gore at the 2015 UN Climate Change Conference (COP21) urging India to switch its energy source from coal to solar to reduce the country's significant greenhouse gas emissions. COP21 is where the Paris Climate Agreement was eventually signed.

Because of his work, Vice President Gore won the very important Nobel Peace Prize in 2007. This is given to people who do something extraordinary for the good of all. He shared the award with the Intergovernmental Panel on Climate Change for "informing the world of the dangers posed by climate change." Lucky for all of us, he's still out there doing this work, fighting every day for our future.

GORE HAS WRITTEN five best-selling books on the climate crisis and its solutions: *Earth in the Balance, An Inconvenient Truth, The Assault on Reason, Our Choice: A Plan to Solve the Climate Crisis,* and *The Future: Six Drivers of Global Change.*

VICE PRESIDENT GORE'S father was a politician, too! He was also a Democratic congressman and senator from Tennessee, where Al Gore grew up and still lives.

ACT LIKE AL GORE

Spread the word about climate change and its solutions. Learn your facts, share them with friends and family to inspire them, and help everyone around you make changes to do their part.

MARINA SILVA

B. 1958

Amazon Rain Forest Protector & Brazilian Politician

As a child living in the Brazilian Amazon, the world's largest tropical rain forest, Marina Silva helped support her large family—she was one of eleven children!—by hunting, fishing, and tapping rubber trees to make rubber. At sixteen, she got sick and had to move to a city in order to get better. There, she learned how to read and eventually went to college. Marina has been fighting to save the rain forest, her native home, ever since—protesting loggers, becoming the first rubber tapper ever elected to Brazil's Senate, and eventually becoming Brazil's minister of the environment from 2003 to 2008. She also ran for president several times, though she has never won.

Depending on where you live, Brazil may seem very far away. But the Amazon rain forest touches your life no matter where you are. By some estimates, 10 percent of our planet's total plant and animal diversity (which is called "biodiversity") is in the Amazon. Rain forests are sometimes called the "lungs of the planet," because they create oxygen and can filter air pollution on a large scale. The Amazon is said to absorb approximately 5 percent of global carbon emissions! Even though the Amazon is so critical to the health of the earth and all its inhabitants, people still cut down its trees for wood and to use the land for farming. It makes zero sense to destroy such an important resource, and it will hurt us in ways we don't even fully understand yet. For instance, many medicines have been discovered using plants that only grow in the rain forest, so when we cut down the forest, we're destroying possible future cures for illness.

In the early 1980s, Marina and an important environmentalist named Chico Mendes began peacefully protesting deforestation and people taking Indigenous land from Native people. Their actions resulted in the protection of millions of acres of tropical forest! But this big win came with horrible loss. Chico was murdered in 1988 because he was trying to protect the Amazon—some people who were making a lot of money by cutting it down didn't want him around anymore. After his death, and despite the danger, Marina bravely continued their work.

Once elected to Brazil's government, Marina shut down many illegal logging operations throughout the Amazon and was able to reduce deforestation by an estimated 80 percent. But in 2019, the Brazilian government released data showing there had been more deforestation in that year alone than in the entire decade, partially due to continued illegal logging and mining that led to giant and destructive fires.

It was also the year Brazil elected Jair Bolsonaro president. He cares more about development than he does about protecting the rain forest. This is bad news. Marina isn't part of President Bolsonaro's government, but she's still promoting sustainable solutions to the climate crisis. At the 2019 UN Climate Conference in Madrid, she apologized to Greta Thunberg on behalf of her country because President Bolsonaro had publicly called Greta names for sympathizing with Indigenous people who have been murdered in Brazil. Hopefully one day soon Brazil will have a president who doesn't bully teenagers and who will once again help save the precious Amazon for all of us on the planet. Maybe Marina could be that president!

MARINA HAS WON many awards for protecting the rain forest, including a Goldman Environmental Prize. She was also named a Champion of the Earth by the United Nation's Environmental Program.

IN 2010, MARINA ran as the Green Party presidential candidate for Brazil and won 19 percent of the vote. Brazil is a very large country, so this means almost 20 million Brazilians voted for her. She now leads another political party called the Sustainability Focus Party.

ACT LIKE MARINA

Join and support organizations working to protect rain forests! Also, if your family uses products that come from a rain forest—like coffee, natural rubber, or vanilla—only buy them from companies that use ingredients grown and harvested in a sustainable way so as not to damage these lungs of our planet.

CHARLES WINDSOR
B. 1948

British Prince & Environmentalist

England has royals—a king and a queen, princes and princesses, and dukes and duchesses! British people on the whole are very interested in their royal family. As a country, they pay lots of attention to what the royals do, whom they marry, what they wear, and especially to what they say. British newspapers, magazines, and television report on royal news constantly. As long as he has this kind of captive audience, Charles Windsor, also known as Prince Charles of Wales, uses it wisely: for more than fifty years, he has been speaking out about environmental issues.

Prince Charles has been concerned about how humans are negatively impacting the environment since he was a child. Ahead of his time, he gave his first environmental speech in 1968. Since the 1990s, he has been raising awareness about actions needed to combat global warming. Royal life comes with many formal rules and regulations, as you can imagine, but Prince Charles still shares openly about the climate crisis and related problems like plastic ocean pollution and the loss of rain forests and all of the diverse plants and animals in them—even when it's unpopular.

Part of a prince's job is traveling the world to visit other heads of state. Wherever Prince Charles goes, including to important conferences and events, he highlights the environment. At home, he even founded his own organic food company, Duchy Originals! They make oat cookies, which are actually called "biscuits" in England. Duchy is the name of Prince Charles's farm at his home estate, which has been organic since 1986. Back then, most people had no idea what organic was, let alone that it meant not spraying gardens with toxic pesticides that would harm farmers and the soil. Prince Charles's farm supplies ingredients for the biscuits.

There's no doubt that princes have big environmental footprints. Imagine any of the royal palaces described or illustrated in your favorite books—they're massive! Large buildings require a lot of energy to heat and operate. But Prince Charles tries to lead by example and publicly details the steps he takes to make his life more earth friendly, so people can try to copy what he does. His homes use some energy from renewable sources, including solar panels. Flying all over the world is obviously not earth friendly, but he tries to travel lighter and

highlight better solutions when he can. In 2020, he arrived at the Fiftieth World Economic Forum in Switzerland in an electric car, for example. Once there, he gave a speech urging business leaders to do their part to help fix the climate crisis. "Global warming, climate change, and the devastating loss of biodiversity are the greatest threats humanity has ever faced," he said there. Many scientists have said the same thing, but oddly fewer people listen to them than they do to a real live prince.

Prince Charles has two adult sons and a growing number of grandchildren. He is concerned for their future. His environmentalism has influenced many, including his sons. One of them, Prince Harry, has also spoken openly about the environmental destruction he sees as he, too, travels the world. We need all our leaders to act now on climate, while there's still time. Royals willing to speak the truth to their powerful peers—which Prince Charles has been doing almost his whole life—are a positive step in the right direction.

· ·

PRINCE CHARLES HAS earned lots of eco-praise: in 2017 he got the Green Carpet Challenge Global Leader of Change Award, in 2012 he was the Lifetime Achievement winner at the seventh International Green Awards, and *Time* magazine has called him a Hero of the Environment.

PRINCE CHARLES HAS said that he talks to the plants at his country home, Highgrove, to help them grow! (For the record, speaking to crops is not necessary for organic certification.)

ACT LIKE PRINCE CHARLES

· ·

Use your audience to raise environmental awareness. Chances are you're not a prince with reporters following your every move, but everyone has a few people willing to listen to them! Speak up at school, at home, and with your friends.

GINA McCARTHY

B. 1954

Career Environmentalist & Warrior

To really protect the earth, we have to strengthen regulations and change laws. Changing laws involves fighting for what you know is right and against people who disagree with you to arrive at compromise. Gina McCarthy, the former head of the US Environmental Protection Agency (EPA) under President Obama and current head of the Natural Resources Defense Council (NRDC), one of America's most important environmental action organizations, likes to fight! She has worked on many laws over the past thirty years, both inside and outside of the government. According to the *New York Times,* she once said, "I cannot shy away from controversy. I don't know if it's my Irish blood, but I love it. I love disagreements. I love the democratic process. If I'm in a room where everybody agrees, I start to nod off."

It can be confusing to understand why Gina even needs to fight. Why would anyone be against good things like clean air and water? The answer is money. People who pollute our air and water make money while doing it, so they don't want laws banning pollution. That's why an energy company that extracts fossil fuel from the earth and sells it around the world fights regulation. Gina's whole career has been about fighting back. At the EPA, she took many steps to make America's climate policy better, like regulating the greenhouse gases that are both warming the earth and polluting the air. She also protected water resources, worked on chemical safety, and helped get the 2015 Paris Climate Agreement signed.

Before joining the EPA and the NRDC, Gina worked on environmental issues in Connecticut as well as in her home state of Massachusetts. She advised five governors there! Her goal, no matter the job, has been to protect our earth. Gina has been called one of the most effective environmental champions alive. Her fighting spirit has impacted the lives of so many people in America and beyond. She is said to be hard working, knowledgeable, and honest. At the NRDC, she's continuing her life's work: safeguarding human health as well as protecting oceans and wildlife, and reducing toxic chemicals in the environment. And, thankfully, she's also fighting to implement solutions for the most important environmental issue of the day: the climate crisis.

AT THE NRDC, Gina has worked to redo a lot of what she already did at the EPA. This is because when Donald Trump became president, he got rid of many of the protections Gina and her staff had put in place for air, water, health, and wildlife. The fight never ends!

THERE'S NO SPECIFIC degree needed if you want a job like Gina's when you grow up, though it does help to do your homework. She studied social anthropology in college at the University of Massachusetts at Boston, then got a graduate degree in environmental health engineering and planning and policy from Tufts University.

ACT LIKE GINA

You've probably seen solar panels on rooftops that take in the sun's energy to make electricity or big turbines that spin when the wind blows so that farmers can heat and light their barns. These technologies are called "renewable energy," and they are amazing because they let us reuse energy that's constantly created in our natural world and don't pollute our air or water or make our planet warmer. Today, people and businesses everywhere are using them more and more—not just because they're good for our health and the environment, but because they create jobs and save money. You can help too by talking about how cool these technologies are to your family, friends, and teachers. When we get everyone in the world to use renewable energy to power their homes, buildings, and businesses, we will all be healthier and safer.

HILDA HEINE

Climate Activist & President of the Marshall Islands

For a long time, climate scientists and activists have been saying that *now* is the time for action. World leaders have to immediately make some big changes in order to slow down the worst effects of a warming climate. If we wait much longer, it will be too late. Actually, there are places in the world where it is already too late. In the Republic of the Marshall Islands, people are being forced to move from their homes because of global warming. Hilda Heine, the Marshallese president from 2016 to 2020, says her people are living the crisis. Because they are some of the first on the planet to be impacted in this way, the whole world has been watching the Marshallese and considering what it means for everyone's future.

The Marshall Islands are a group of low-lying volcanic islands in the Pacific Ocean. Global warming is causing sea level to rise. The biggest contributor to sea level rise is melting ice— as temperatures climb around the world, glaciers in the Arctic and Antarctic are melting faster and faster, putting more and more water into the oceans. It's hard to imagine what sea level rise looks like, especially if you live far from an ocean. For the people of the Republic of Marshall Islands, it's simple: it means flooding. It also means they don't have fresh drinking water, because when the sea level rises in a place as low as the Marshall Islands, salt water gets into fresh water and makes it unsafe to drink. To add to the problem, they also have severe drought. Many Marshallese are now climate refugees, moving to unflooded countries with drinkable water. Others are staying put and doing what they can as the water rises. As glaciers at the North and South Poles continue to melt, other low-lying countries will meet similar fates, and so will many cities on coasts all over the world.

President Heine grew up on the Marshall Islands but went to college and graduate school in the United States. She returned home to become a teacher and then rose through the ranks as a school administrator. After working as a college president, she entered politics and became the nation's minister of education before becoming president. Heine didn't study to be a global climate justice leader. Being president of a nation that she has said is "facing death row" motivated her to act! In her country, she worked on creating a climate adaption plan that included raising some islands higher above sea level so their culture could live on. She also spoke with

other countries about immigration and whether they would welcome climate refugees, to guide her citizens through the life changes they face.

President Heine has used her front-row seat at the climate crisis to speak out and ask world leaders to take stronger action. She has shared the story of her people at climate conferences around the world. She has urged the worst-polluting countries to do better and asked rich nations to do more. After the yearly UN climate conference—called COP for short—took place in Madrid in 2019, Heine wrote on Twitter, "If it was not for the Marshall Islands and our #HighAmbitionCoalition, there would have been an even weaker outcome at #COP25Madrid. While we should be disappointed with the behavior of some big emitters, we should be proud we helped protect against an even weaker outcome."

World leaders need to continue to do better when it comes to the climate crisis. President Heine set a great example, publicizing her homeland's vulnerable position to spread awareness. The current reality of the Marshall Islands is very upsetting, but thanks to Heine, it may end up being part of the solution we all seek.

PRESIDENT HEINE WAS the first female president of the Marshall Islands—and the first female leader in the entire Pacific. She's also the first person from the Marshall Islands to earn a doctorate degree.

NEARLY 40 PERCENT of the world lives by water in a coastal area. The most recent predictions by the Intergovernmental Panel on Climate Change are that within the next hundred years, sea level could rise so much that it would flood coasts and the people who live on them all over the globe.

ACT LIKE HILDA HEINE

Look for a local grassroots group committed to climate action and join them. If there isn't a group, create one!

VICKI BUCK

Politician & Entrepreneur

When Vicki Buck was eighteen, she became a politician—a councillor, or a member of her city council. She liked being able to enact real change in her community as an elected official, versus trying to change one thing at a time as a private citizen. She stuck to it and eventually served three terms, from 1989 to 1998, as the mayor of her hometown, Christchurch, the third-biggest city in New Zealand.

Vicki is a curious person who is constantly learning and finding new interests, so, after her time as mayor, she got involved in lots of things outside politics, too. She was especially interested in environmentalism, so she joined forces with various companies trying to combat climate change. One was focused on wind farms, which produce renewable energy from wind. Another was a climate-themed website. A third was trying to reduce methane, a potent greenhouse gas that comes from raising animals like beef cattle, among other sources.

A fourth, super-interesting company was called Aquaflow Bionomic Corporation. Its goal was to make earth-friendly renewable biofuel for cars and airplanes out of wild algae that grows in sewage ponds! Biofuel—which is basically fuel made from plants—sounds great, but it all depends on what plant is used to make it. Corn is a common biofuel crop, but growing it for fuel can take food away from people. Plus, forests are often cut down to clear land to plant the corn, which is bad because trees help clean the air, among other benefits. Corn is also typically sprayed with a lot of earth-unfriendly pesticides. But wild algae biofuel doesn't have any of these problems. It's made from waste, burns cleaner than gasoline, and doesn't contribute as much to global warming. Airplane fuel made from pond scum is a pretty cool idea! It got a lot of attention. In 2008, the *Guardian* newspaper even named Vicki one of fifty people who could change the world.

Busy with biofuel and more, Vicki felt like she was done with politics. But then there were earthquakes in Christchurch. Seeing their impact on her city pulled her back to government work. By 2013, she was a councillor again. This time in office, Vicki, based on her experience as both a politician and with environmental businesses, was much more aware of how dangerous the climate crisis was for all inhabitants of our planet—humans and all species. She led Christchurch's Innovation and Sustainability Committee, determined to tackle what she has called the hugest issue of our time. Her committee focused on water quality, electric vehicles, and creating safer bike lanes to reduce driving. Her goal is to leave the planet better than she found it.

MAKING BIOFUEL FROM algae basically means making it from poop! Here's how: When human waste gets flushed down a toilet, it travels to sewage ponds, where it's cleaned and turned into wastewater that then flows into rivers and oceans. Algae is formed in sewage water when it's exposed to sunlight and carbon dioxide. That's what the Aquaflow Bionomic Corporation was turning into fuel. Talk about a renewable resource!

VICKI DOESN'T CONSIDER herself an eco-role model (even though she is!), but she always does these three things: she walks a lot, uses public transportation, and avoids plastic bags.

ACT LIKE VICKI

It doesn't matter what action you start with—whether it's a change of something you eat, use, or travel in, or a political action that gets others changing. It's just important to do it—make a start and keep going. All of us now are the last generation with a chance to impact climate change, and so it's up to all of us. And it's urgent.

ANGELA MERKEL

Policy Leader & Climate Chancellor

Climate activists today are constantly asking government leaders to listen to the world's scientists and to act on their research urgently to protect the planet. It's pretty rare that these leaders are scientists themselves. German chancellor Angela Merkel is an exception. (In Germany, the chancellor is the head of the government.) She studied physics and chemistry at school—she has a PhD—and worked as a chemist before becoming a politician. She's even married to a scientist. So Merkel understands more than most that today's need for climate action is based on concrete scientific evidence.

Chancellor Merkel first became Germany's environment minister in 1994. Even back then, when she attended the first UN Climate Conference (COP), she was already trying to get world leaders to reduce greenhouse gas emissions to avoid climate change. Merkel became the first woman chancellor of Germany—and one of the most powerful leaders in Europe—in 2005. To this day, she continues to demand climate action at international conferences and gatherings. Her focus on the issue has earned her the nickname "Climate Chancellor." She was at the COP in 2009 in Copenhagen when international leaders failed to agree on goals for reducing emissions. She was also at the COP in 2015 in Paris when they succeeded. Her hard work for "ambitious, comprehensive, fair and binding" goals helped get the Paris Climate Agreement signed.

People all over the world like to complain about their politicians—even when they're pretty good. Some Germans wish the Climate Chancellor had done as much climate work at home as she did globally. But Merkel has said she believes a politician's job is to consider all options in any given situation to figure out what steps are even possible, well before rolling out changes. This approach rarely results in fast action, especially when it comes to the climate, which can be frustrating. Germany has already missed deadlines on some of its own emissions reduction plans, and the country still struggles with its use of coal, a dirty energy source that pollutes the air. The country set goals it has promised to meet by 2050, which include cutting greenhouse gases, using less energy overall, and shifting to more renewable

energy. Meanwhile, Germans, like everyone in Europe, are already living with the effects of the climate crisis, including heat waves.

When President Donald Trump made the decision to remove the United States from the 2015 Paris Climate Agreement, Chancellor Merkel denounced it to the world as "very regrettable." She also urged the global leaders who remained committed to the agreement to move forward on implementing it. Amazingly, there are still people spreading the lie that global warming isn't real. This makes Merkel's work that much more important worldwide, even though she is not seeking reelection in 2021. The world hasn't yet slowed or stopped global emissions to ensure a future where today's kids—that's you!—and their children will live well. Having a strong global leader like Merkel—who has been loudly and consistently saying for decades that the climate crisis is real, that it's human-made, and that we have to listen to scientists and do everything possible to overcome it now—is still as important as ever.

AS A SCIENTIST, Merkel once coauthored a paper entitled "Vibrational Properties of Surface Hydroxyls: Nonempirical Model Calculations Including Anharmonicities." If you don't know what a hydroxyl is, you're not alone! You'll probably learn about this chemical group involving hydrogen and oxygen when you take chemistry in school.

MERKEL IS ONE of the most important women in the world, but she has hobbies just like anyone else. She is said to like soccer, hiking, gardening, classical music including opera, and cooking. She also likes to bake, especially plum cake. One thing she reportedly does not like? Dogs!

ACT LIKE ANGELA MERKEL

Study science and always pay attention to scientific evidence. Use what you learn in all areas of your life to make a difference—maybe even as a politician.

VANDANA SHIVA B. 1952

Scientist & Non-GMO Activist

Have you ever seen the label "non-GMO" at the supermarket? GMO stands for **genetically modified organism.** Seeds used to grow GMO foods are modified—or changed—in a laboratory. Companies modify plants to fight off pests and so they can survive challenges like drought and cold weather. GMO seeds help industrial agriculture companies grow more plants, feed more people, and earn more money. Sounds okay in theory, but it may not be safe to eat food grown from seeds that have been injected in a lab with genes from various sources to make them poisonous to insects and more. Vandana Shiva, a physicist, is one of the loudest voices in the world saying GMOs are unsafe. She advises governments across the globe about the risks of genetic modification.

A non-GMO label on food means it has *not* been genetically modified. Depending on where you live, the food you eat might already be modified! Although many countries have banned GMOs, America has not, despite activists requesting a ban since GMOs were first widely planted in the United States in 1996. Typical **genetically modified foods** include corn and soy, two ingredients that show up in many, many packaged foods.

As GMO seeds are becoming increasingly widespread, non-GMO, or traditional, seeds are going extinct. To keep non-GMO seeds and farming traditions alive, Vandana helped establish a farm in India called Navdanya. There, she teaches farmers about growing, saving, sharing, and protecting non-GMO seeds. She educates students—a mix of global citizens, local farmers, and schoolchildren—about organic farming and the importance of biodiversity, or growing and protecting a wide variety of plants. When we don't grow these plants and save their seeds, we lose the plants forever. In 2018, the German Federal Office for Agriculture and Food said that 75 percent of vegetables grown between 1836 and 1956 no longer exist! This is alarming news—even if you don't like vegetables. To grow more varieties, we need seeds. Through Navdanya, Vandana has set up more than a hundred seed banks to date for farmers to store collected seeds. She has already conserved thousands of varieties of rice, wheat, and other species.

We all depend on the earth. As our global population grows, everyone will need to eat. There are two main models of agriculture that can be used to feed people, and they are total opposites. There's industrial agriculture: growing food from GMO seeds owned by large companies, which requires harmful chemicals and lots of water. Or there's sustainable agriculture: growing food from traditional native seeds on biodiverse farms, which requires less water and no harmful chemicals. Vandana says sustainable agriculture is the one true answer to the future of food and nutrition, and she has devoted her life to fighting for it. This is why *Forbes* magazine named her one of the most powerful women in the world and *Time* magazine called her an environmental hero!

AS A CHILD, Vandana spent time in India's Himalayan forest and has said nature is her best teacher. Her father was a forestry government official and her mom was a farmer. Her local forest inspired her to become an activist; she joined a movement to protect it when its trees were being cut down for wood. Deforestation harms animals and local people, as well as the soil, water, and air.

BRITAIN'S PRINCE CHARLES has a sculpture of Vandana in his garden! She has advised him on sustainable agriculture.

ACT LIKE VANDANA

Look for and ask your parents to buy non-GMO foods. Plant your own biodiverse garden and learn how to save your seeds from one growing season to the next. Share your seeds with friends. If a pest or insect starts nibbling your crops, use organic methods to fight back.

ALICE WATERS   B. 1944

Chef & Food Activist

Farmers' markets in America are pretty easy to find these days, especially if you live in a city or a suburban town. And lots of restaurants use words like "local" and "organic" on their menus. But back in 1971, when Alice Waters opened her restaurant, Chez Panisse, in Berkeley, California, neither was typical. Alice is considered the founder of the farm-to-table movement. This literally means serving food from farms at your table. Her interest in buying food that is in season directly from local farmers has influenced many chefs and home cooks. She has also educated countless children about growing and cooking flavorful food— and fed them!—through her Edible Schoolyard Project, which launched in 1995 at Berkeley's Martin Luther King Jr. Middle School. Many schools across the United States now have edible gardens, maybe even yours.

Alice didn't particularly love food as a kid. She has said her family's cooking was uninspiring. The food revolution of the 1940s and 1950s was about saving people time—that's when canned items and fast, frozen, ready-to-eat meals became popular. Her parents grew some food in a backyard garden but stopped canning it because store-bought items were easier and faster. Little did anyone know that Alice would grow up to start the next food revolution that campaigned against this exact fast food!

During college, Alice traveled to France to study and had a food awakening. She still speaks fondly of buying warm French baguettes and eating them with incredible butter and apricot jam. She also talks about tiny wild French strawberries; she was amazed by their intense flavor, by learning that they had to be handpicked in the woods, and that they grow for only a short window of time every year. Alice was charmed by little restaurants all over Paris and by walking through beautiful markets on the way to school. She loved seeing the vibrant vegetables and live fish, all grown or caught locally. This was nothing like the American supermarkets she had experienced.

After college, Alice taught preschool briefly. In her spare time, she cooked French food for her friends and eventually opened a small restaurant—Chez Panisse. She served only one set menu each day, not a bunch of options, all made from local, seasonal food grown with

care for the earth—and not sprayed with unsafe chemicals. To find these kinds of ingredients, she became friends with local farmers. Chez Panisse wound up being one of the most famous restaurants in America. It has won many awards, and Alice has written several cookbooks, plus a memoir: *Coming to My Senses: The Making of a Counterculture Cook.*

Today, Alice's influence on American food is everywhere. The fact that there are more people buying directly from small farmers is great. Unfortunately, though, some large corporations and chain restaurants now use terms Alice made popular like "local" and "organic" in misleading ways on their menus and food packaging, trying to get people to buy their products without actually using local or organic ingredients. This is one of the reasons Alice says she hasn't been in a conventional grocery store in more than twenty-five years! When you support and know your farmers directly, you become an important part of how they grow tasty food that's good for them, the earth, and all of us.

THERE'S A POSTER of Alice's food philosophy that gets shared a lot on social media. It reads, "Eat seasonally. Eat locally and sustainably. Shop at farmers' markets. Plant a garden. Conserve, compost, and recycle. Cook simply, engaging all your senses. Set the table with care and respect. Eat together. Food is precious."

ALICE ONCE FAMOUSLY asked the US government for three things: to plant an organic garden on the White House grounds, to hire a staff chef educated about local and organic food, and for all public school students to be taught about sustainable agriculture. She got two out of three! The White House garden and chef lasted through several different presidents—Democratic and Republican. To date, there is no national sustainable agriculture curriculum. But we can keep trying!

ACT LIKE ALICE

Follow Alice's food philosophy to join her delicious revolution! Cook and share family meals made with local ingredients. Plant a garden and eat what you grow. If you mainly shop at grocery stores, give farmers' markets a try.

WILL ALLEN

B. 1949

Urban Farmer & Food Justice Activist

Okra is Will Allen's favorite vegetable. What's yours? If you've never had okra, it's worth trying. Will is a former basketball player who became an urban farmer. Farming may not sound as cool as professional sports, but Will's journey from hoops to crops has been revolutionary!

In 1993, Will bought two acres with old greenhouses in a neighborhood of Milwaukee, Wisconsin, that had no shops selling affordable fruits or vegetables. People who lived there had to travel many miles to get to a grocery store. When you have no way to find healthy food near where you live, you have to eat what's available at convenience stores and fast-food restaurants, which isn't always the healthiest. Will believes that when you eat better, you feel better, and you behave better. So he set out to grow better food for this neighborhood and to create a community. His urban farming project became an organization called Growing Power.

Will had farmed before Growing Power. He grew up the son of a sharecropper in Maryland. Sharecropping, which has roots in slavery, means growing food on land you don't own. Sharecroppers share the crops they grow as payment for using their landlord's land. When Will was a kid, the word "organic" wasn't used, but even then he was interested in aspects of organic farming, like how compost adds nutrients to the soil.

Youth education was a big part of Growing Power. Some of the students Will trained had gotten into trouble with the law. Will used farming to help empower them and to boost their confidence. He taught kids how to make compost and to grow vegetables and flowers, which they then sold. He even taught them how to raise fish to fertilize Growing Power's plants in a unique and sustainable way. Will had his students plant flowers in empty paved lots, discouraging crimes from taking place there and helping to beautify the community. As the farm grew, it became a training hub—people came from all over the world to learn about urban farming! Will kept adding to the farm, too, expanding with new greenhouses and animals including chickens, goats, and bees.

Will's farm was so influential that in 2008, he won a MacArthur "Genius Grant"—a very important prize given for creativity. Magazines and newspapers wrote articles about him, and First Lady Michelle Obama invited him to be part of her Let's Move! campaign.

He also wrote a book called *The Good Food Revolution: Growing Healthy Food, People, and Communities.*

Growing Power closed in 2017, but its impact has been monumental. It lives on in Will's many students who started similar farms in their own neighborhoods, offering both training and healthy food to communities that previously had neither. Turning empty city lots into farms and education hubs with access to nutritious food has changed the lives of many kids for the better, especially young people of color. Will founded Growing Power to get back to his farming roots and to improve the diet—and health—of just one urban community. Instead, he wound up starting an international urban farming movement. Today, urban farms with education centers are more common—and access to healthy, affordable food grown without chemicals that are bad for the environment has expanded widely, too. We can thank Will for that.

THE NEXT GENERATION of Will's farmers has bloomed: Erika Allen, his daughter, leads the Urban Growers Collective, a Chicago organization that focuses on growing food and expanding food access as well as on educating and empowering young people of color.

FARMING IS MORE challenging than basketball! Allen has said, "To be a sustainable farmer and grow without chemicals is harder than being a professional athlete."

ACT LIKE WILL

Grow food to grow community. What you learn from your parents as a kid may help you change the world one day. Also, eat your okra.

CARLO PETRINI

Activist & Slow Food Founder

If someone asked you where pollution comes from, you'd probably answer power plants and cars. And you'd be right! But another leading cause of the climate crisis is food. Agricultural pollution doesn't come from the garden in your backyard where your family grows a few herbs and vegetables. And it doesn't even really come from small local farms. It's from huge modern industrial farms that use toxic fertilizers and pesticides that pollute our water, soil, and air. Raising large numbers of animals for meat is another big culprit; concentrated livestock farms pollute waterways and release tons of methane, one of the greenhouse gases responsible for warming our planet. Carlo Petrini has spent decades helping people grow, make, and enjoy food that pollutes our world less.

When the American fast-food chain McDonald's opened its first restaurant in Italy in the 1980s, Carlo and other food activists responded by starting Slow Food, an organization promoting locally sourced food and traditional cooking. To protest that first Italian McDonald's, they served pasta in the plaza out front. Pasta is a traditional "slow food" they love—and the total opposite of fast food.

Carlo grew up in an Italian town where social time—when people are not at work or school—was all about shopping for, cooking, and sharing food. He has childhood memories of his grandmother teaching him about Italian culture by lovingly cooking for him. Back then, people mostly bought food directly from local farmers, butchers, and cheese makers. Today, we shop for packaged foods at supermarkets and have no idea who grew it or where it came from. Although this kind of industrial food has fed a lot of people across the world, it's not as nutritious as the local food it replaced. And the way we make it is harming the earth, animals, and humans.

To grow large amounts of food quickly, you need synthetic pesticides to kill the insects that can harm the plants and fertilizer to make the crops grow faster. You also need a tremendous amount of water. Many places in the world are suffering from drought—there isn't enough water for people to drink, let alone farm with. And yet Carlo has said 76 percent of all water in the world is being used for industrial farming! Fast farming also changes food. This can create

health problems. People today have allergies that weren't common when Carlo was a child. And diseases related to diet, like diabetes and obesity, are on the rise, even for young people.

Slow Food has come a long way since its McDonald's pasta protest! It's now a global movement with over a million supporters across more than 160 countries working to preserve delicious traditional flavors. Thanks to Carlo and Slow Food, produce from small farms and other local alternatives to industrial food are making a comeback. Slow Food also promotes the pleasure and joy of eating meals together with the people we love. Carlo believes love is the future of food. Love is what will push back against the modern large-scale farming that is making us sicker and warming our earth. Love is what will help us live in balance with nature and protect our planet by embracing slower food for all.

SMALL FARMERS AND fishermen from all over the planet come together to talk about their concerns and solutions at a yearly Slow Food event in Italy called Terra Madre (that means "Mother Earth" in Italian).

SLOW FOOD CHAPTERS are in cities and towns all over the world. Some chapters keep lists of local restaurants cooking traditional food. When you're traveling to a new place and looking for somewhere to eat, ask your parents to check out Slow Food's "Snail of Approval" recommendations.

ACT LIKE CARLO

Saving biodiversity is as simple as eating. Know the story of who produced your food, ask for the names of the vegetables you see, discover the way they've been cultivated, and choose the ones that traveled the least from farm to your fork. Knowing the story behind the food on your plate and eating locally and diversified is the best way to enjoy your meals and protect the environment, nourishing yourself and the planet at the same time.

WINONA LaDUKE

B. 1959

Environmentalist & Political Activist

Winona LaDuke does so many things to safeguard the earth, it's hard to pick just one to talk about! For starters, she works on all aspects of sustainable agriculture—with a specific focus on protecting the foods her Native American ancestors have been growing on their land for many years from genetic modification. A genetically modified (GM) plant has had its natural DNA changed so it can be grown faster, often with earth-unfriendly chemicals. Winona is also a proponent of clean and renewable energy, which comes from resources like wind and sunlight, plus rain and tides. She also organizes people to stop giant pipelines from being built to transport dirty fossil fuels like oil and natural gas across land, including Native American land. See? She does a *lot*!

To accomplish all of this, Winona runs various organizations. There's Honor the Earth, which focuses on climate change, among other issues. White Earth Land Recovery Project, which she founded on the White Earth Reservation, where she lives, addresses food and renewable energy, and is also devoted to reclaiming land the US government promised to Native Americans years ago but never gave them. Winona has won many important awards for her wide-ranging environmental and climate justice work, including the Reebok Human Rights Award and *Ms.* Woman of the Year. She's often invited to give speeches at big conferences, too.

Here's a story Winona tells at some conferences, about wild rice and her people. She's a member of the Mississippi Band Anishinaabeg, a tribe that has always cared for rice beds in the lakes on their land in northern Minnesota. Historically, when it was time to harvest the rice, they would start by offering thanks for it. Then they'd harvest hundreds of pounds of rice, dry it, parch it over a fire, and dance on it to separate the hulls. Next, they'd do a process called winnowing to remove the hulls. After a harvest, they have a big celebratory feast—a thanksgiving. For many years, the tribe has traded the wild rice they harvest, selling it for money and exchanging it for other items they need.

Then, non-Native people figured out how to grow rice in paddies using chemicals and fertilizers. Their harvest is industrial. They drain the paddies and use a machine called a combine harvester instead of their hands to harvest and process the rice. This is faster than the Native way, but the chemicals harm waterways and wildlife, the rice is not as nutritious, and commercial rice production interferes with the tribe's ability to earn money. They can't compete, especially with GMO rice.

Winona has fought this industrial version of rice for a long time—just one of her many battles. Her whole family has riced for generations. Winona believes "wild" should mean something special. She has said, "Nothing gets solved overnight. It takes years to solve these issues." This is just one example of how modern-day practices are harming our earth, undermining Native Americans' way of life, and contributing to global problems. That's why Winona is still fighting, for her people, for the earth, and for all of us.

WINONA WAS A two-time vice presidential candidate for the Green Party. The two best-known political parties in the United States are the Democrats and Republicans, but there are other parties, too. She didn't win, but her campaigns helped her share her messages with many people all over the country.

WINONA'S FATHER WAS a movie actor in Westerns as well as an activist fighting for Native American causes.

ACT LIKE WINONA

Be the ancestor your descendants will thank. Get involved to protect our land, water, air, and food for today, tomorrow, and future generations.

PETE SEEGER

B. 1919–D. 2014

Folk Singer & Legendary Activist

Folk singer Pete Seeger used music—his banjo and his voice—to push for social change. He lived a long, full life, singing through many decades about the issues of the day. In the 1940s and 1950s, he sang about the rights of workers. In the 1960s, he sang for civil rights and against the Vietnam War. In the 1970s, Pete started singing about bringing people together to protect the earth.

You have probably heard some of Pete's songs. He had many! Some are still sung by kids today, taught in school music classes or shared around summer campfires, like "If I Had a Hammer" and "Where Have All the Flowers Gone?" A few of Pete's songs became anthems for the social justice movements he cared so much about. If you've ever been to a climate march or an Earth Day celebration, chances are his music was played between speeches and chants. Pete said he was never interested in being famous, but he sure used his fame well to spread the word about environmental issues.

In the late 1940s, Pete bought seventeen acres of land near the Hudson River in Beacon, New York, about an hour north of New York City. He and his wife built a cabin there using instructions from library books! They lived there the rest of his life. In the 1960s, he got involved in efforts to save the polluted Hudson River, which was filled with sewage and toxic chemicals. He put on a concert called the Clearwater Festival with other musicians to raise money to build a 106-foot sailboat named the *Clearwater*, modeled on sloops that used to sail the Hudson. The boat is now a floating classroom and a symbol of effective grassroots action. Pete and his wife launched an environmental organization, which they also called Clearwater, and now the festival has become an annual, internationally known folk music event. It raises money for the organization, which fights for environmental and social justice. Pete's antipollution and educational work continues to inspire many environmentalists far beyond the Hudson Valley.

Protesting for justice is hard work. There are many ups and downs, emotions and setbacks. There are wins, but sometimes too few, especially when it comes to the environment. One thing people always say about Pete is that he was upbeat and optimistic, despite all he was fighting for. Pete's protest songs are incredibly moving. They're funny and gorgeous and

sad and lovely. The lyrics feel as important today as they did in the 1970s. Listen to them, and see if they motivate you as they have so many environmental activists before you. The power of music to mobilize and change people's minds is amazing—and Pete was, too.

....

MUSIC RUNS IN Pete's family. His father was a musicologist, and his mom was a concert violinist. His wife was a musician, too, as are his kids and some of his grandkids!

FOLK MUSICIANS OFTEN sing songs written by others. Pete did—and made many popular, including "This Land Is Your Land"; "We Shall Overcome," the anthem of the civil rights movement; and a song called "Garbage," written in 1969. Its lyrics are still relevant today: "Oh, Garbage, garbage, garbage, garbage / We're filling up the seas with garbage / What will we do when there's no place left / To put all the garbage?"

ACT LIKE PETE
....

Sing for what you believe in, for your whole long life. Pete sang until he died at the age of ninety-four. He once said, "My job is to show folks there's a lot of good music in this world, and if used right it may help to save the planet."

YVON CHOUINARD

B. 1938

Rock Climber & Businessman

As a kid, Yvon Chouinard basically lived outdoors. He zoomed around on his bike, skipped high school dances to catch frogs, and even snuck onto private property to fish. At fourteen, as a member of the Southern California Falconry Club, he learned how to rappel down cliffs. As he grew older, his adventures grew, too: climbing rocks in state parks, skiing down volcanoes in South America, surfing all over the world. He almost died once in an avalanche!

These kinds of outdoor adventures require gear that works well and isn't too heavy. Yvon didn't like what was available, so he made his own. He learned how to forge metal into pitons—objects that climbers stick into rock for support—plus other tools. This became his first business, Chouinard Equipment. When he realized his pitons were damaging the rock he loved to climb because they had to be hammered into it, Yvon came up with an alternative, which could be wedged into already existing cracks in the rock. Problem solved. This was the first of many earth-friendly changes he made to his designs.

Yvon never much liked businesspeople, but soon he became a famous one himself. He launched a company called Patagonia in 1973 with the goal of making better outdoor clothing. Instead of traditional fabrics like cotton and wool, Patagonia tried out synthetic ones like fleece and polypropylene, which don't absorb moisture and keep people dry, warm, and protected from harsh weather without too many bulky layers. Lots of clothes today are made from fleece, but it was unusual back then. The company took off! Patagonia is now one of the best-known outdoor clothing and gear brands in the world.

Yvon wanted to give back to the earth that he loved and that his company helped people explore. To do its part, Patagonia collaborates with and donates money to environmental organizations. As early as the 1970s, the company worked to help protect a river near its California office, where dams were built that were ruining fish and wildlife habitat.

When he started Patagonia, Yvon wasn't aware that a clothing company could harm the earth, but soon he learned that the process of making clothes can have a big impact on the environment. Over many years, he has worked to make clothing manufacturing less harmful. He shares what he learns with other clothing brands, too, so they can make similar

117

changes. Patagonia tries to use earth-friendlier fabrics, like recycled instead of new polyester, which is made from petroleum. The company switched to using organic cotton, too, because it is grown without unsafe synthetic pesticides. It switched its fabric dyes to lessen water pollution. Patagonia has struggled to replace the chemicals it uses to make gear and clothing waterproof with safer versions, but is trying. It also tries to keep customers from throwing their products out and into a landfill by fixing broken zippers, allowing people to return old gear for store credit, and reselling used gear. Companies will need to take sustainable steps like these if we're going to save the planet. With Patagonia, Yvon has become one of the most important leaders pushing to change how businesses can address environmental harm.

Yvon's wild excursions have taken him all over the world. His most recent adventure is food. He has said agriculture is the worst villain in climate change, which means it also offers the best opportunity to make a real difference. If Yvon can help change how people eat the way he changed what we wear, the world will be a better place.

YVON CALLS CONVENTIONAL cotton the "greatest environmental evildoer" of any fiber. According to Patagonia, 16 percent of all pesticides used in the world are for growing conventional cotton. These chemicals pollute soil and water, and they harm the health of cotton workers. Certified organic cotton is made without these chemicals. It also uses way less water and causes less air pollution. So, buying items made from organic rather than conventional cotton can make a big impact on the world!

WHEN YVON WAS eighteen, he spent an entire summer climbing, living on just fifty cents a day. With so little money, he bought cans of dented cat food to eat! It wasn't very tasty. He also ate squirrel and porcupine.

ACT LIKE YVON

Get outside and have an adventure. And use your power! When people demand better and more earth-friendly products, businesses must change. Buy only what you need, preferably stuff that will last a long time. Repair items you already own.

MARK RUFFALO

B. 1967

Actor & Environmental Advocate

If you've ever seen any of *The Avengers* movies, you know Mark Ruffalo—he's the actor who plays the Hulk. In the United States, where Mark lives and works, being a Hollywood star means people are interested in your life beyond the characters you play. They want to know about your family, your kids (Mark has three), and even what you think about politicians. The attention can be overwhelming. But if you have something to say and you want a lot of people to listen, being a celebrity makes it much easier to get your message out there.

Mark's message is about protecting the earth. In recent years, he has devoted a lot of time to fighting fracking. This is a way of getting a kind of fossil fuel called natural gas out of underground rock formations where it's trapped. Fracking involves injecting chemicals, sand, and a lot of water at a very high pressure deep into the earth to break the rock. This releases the natural gas so it can be captured and used. It also does bad things to the environment.

Mark lives far from Hollywood on a former dairy farm near the Delaware River in New York State. He grew up close to a forest in Wisconsin, which he has said he loved, and his kids are also being raised in nature. His house happens to be built on top of the kind of rock where natural gas is found. When energy companies were trying to get permission to frack near him in New York, Mark got involved with other "fracktivists" and started protesting fracking. They feared fracking chemicals would contaminate the air and the water and make people sick—which has happened in nearby Pennsylvania and other places that allow fracking. It was an ugly and long battle. After careful consideration of the science and because of health risks, New York State decided to ban fracking in 2014. A huge victory!

Because he's famous, Mark was able to get people's attention, including that of politicians, who don't ordinarily give much thought to natural gas extraction methods or wonder about what chemicals might be used in fracking fluid. Beyond fighting fracking, Mark, a devoted environmentalist, also works on creating awareness about how pipelines that transport oil can harm land, wildlife, and humans; climate change; shifting to renewable energy like solar and wind; and the need for clean water for all.

In 2019, Mark's acting overlapped with his environmentalism when he starred in the movie *Dark Waters,* which is based on a true story. He played a lawyer fighting a big chemical company that poisoned the water of thousands of people in West Virginia with PFAS chemicals (this stands for per- and polyfluoroalkyl substances). PFAS chemicals are used to do stuff like make jackets waterproof and carpets stainproof. PFAS are also found in nonstick pans; they make the pan surface slippery so you don't have to add oil when you cook and what makes it easier to clean, too. This all sounds good, but it's not—PFAS have been linked to health problems, including cancer, and it sticks around in your body and in nature for a really long time.

Mark learned so much about PFAS working on *Dark Waters* that he spoke in front of Congress, asking the US government to regulate the chemicals. He testified, "I have been gifted with this outsize media coverage, celebrity. . . . I want to give people the voice that don't have a voice." That makes Mark a real-life superhero: the Earth Avenger!

MARK HAS SAID his kids inspired him to fight fracking. He didn't want them to be hurt by the toxic chemicals used in the process.

MARK HAS RECEIVED many acting awards and some for environmental advocacy, too, including a Global Green Millennium Award and a Meera Gandhi Giving Back Foundation Award.

ACT LIKE MARK

Lend your voice to others! Use whatever audience you have available to you—even if it's just your parents and friends—and speak out loudly about the environmental issues that you think are important.

WILLIAM McDONOUGH   B. 1951

Architect & Sustainability Visionary

When William McDonough was a kid growing up in Japan, he saw that his family's sewage was being reused as fertilizer at farms that grew food. The idea of reusing waste for something new—growing food—instead of getting rid of it like garbage, stuck with him. Many years later, after he studied to become an architect, this simple cycle of reuse from his child-hood inspired him to have a big idea. He decided to reinvent the way people design and create everything—from the buildings we live in to the products we use daily.

The basics of William's idea are this: Humans create too much waste, but in nature, there is no waste. Leaves that fall off a tree aren't waste; they feed nutrients to the soil. And think about the water cycle you learned about in school—not a drop of waste! William thought that if how we design items could imitate nature, where everything is reused, the waste that clogs our landfills as garbage and poisons our earth would get drastically reduced. Designing like nature is a revolutionary concept! William put this big idea into practice through his work as an architect and a **sustainability** consultant.

In 2002, William cowrote a book (with Michael Braungart, a German chemist) called *Cradle to Cradle: Remaking the Way We Make Things.* In the book, they explain that most products are born, used, and then thrown out—that's cradle to grave. For a product to be cradle to cradle means you can take its parts and make new things out of them instead of sending them to a landfill at the end of their useful life. Cradle to cradle is designing a product with its full life cycle in mind. That's why William earned the nickname "the father of the circular economy."

Today, companies can have their products—anything from tape to building supply materials—certified cradle to cradle (C2C). Just like the label "organic" tells people the food they're buying was grown a certain way, the C2C label tells consumers what they're buying was designed for reuse—like in nature! In 2018, the Dutch clothing store C&A even came out with C2C-certified jeans. These were really complicated to make. William worked with C&A to find solutions to many design problems. They wound up using organic cotton and sewing thread grown without toxic pesticides, dyes made from plant waste so they don't pollute our waterways, and renewable energy for the manufacturing process. They shared what they learned making these jeans with other brands in the fashion industry so they, too, could make similarly sustainable clothing and have the biggest possible impact. Sharing is caring!

Williams's work goes far beyond clothing. He has been the architect of many well-known buildings, including NASA's sustainability base—it's like a space station on earth. He has even helped design entire cities!

Reusing waste and making it valuable for future generations, as well as finding ways to make new stuff with zero waste, have revolutionized the design world and reduced the environmental impact of both buildings and everyday products. That's why *Time* magazine named William a "Hero for the Planet." William has credited that first cycle of reuse he saw during his childhood in Japan (when, as he says, "our poop became food") as his inspiration for much of his incredible work as an adult. You just never know what will inspire you to think outside the box and protect our earth!

WILLIAM HAS EARNED many awards for his cradle-to-cradle design, including the Presidential Award for Sustainable Development, the EPA Presidential Green Chemistry Challenge Award, and a National Design Award for exemplary achievement in environmental design.

EVERYTHING WILLIAM DOES is a cradle-to-cradle experiment—even the paper his book was printed on! The pages of *Cradle to Cradle* don't come from trees but instead are a paper-like polypropylene plastic. If your local recycling system recycles that type of plastic, the book can technically be fully reused.

ACT LIKE WILLIAM

Imitate nature to help save it. Rethink the ways things have always been done to see if you can improve them. Share your ideas with others—and always have fun!

GABRIEL OROZCO

B. 1962

Artist & Lover of Found Objects

Have you ever gone to a beach and seen plastic garbage all over? A big reason it's there is that when people throw garbage "away," there's actually no such place. Here's the truth: all garbage remains right here on earth! So bottles wind up on our beaches; plastic bags wrap around tree branches, high up where the wind takes them; and litter is everywhere—from coastlines to parks to forests.

Gabriel Orozco is an internationally known artist who makes art from found objects, including litter he comes across walking down the street or out in nature. Once he neatly arranged more than 1,200 pieces of trash he found at Isla Arena, a Mexican wildlife reserve, on the floor at the Deutsche Guggenheim Museum in Berlin, Germany (he later recreated this piece at the Guggenheim in New York City). On the walls next to this trash art installation, he hung a dozen very large photographs of pieces of the garbage. Several art critics who attended this show wrote articles about how the installation, entitled *Sandstars*, forced museum audiences to confront the effects of worldwide garbage pollution directly. By arranging litter on a museum floor, Gabriel got people talking about a problem they don't usually discuss.

Gabriel grew up in Mexico surrounded by artists, including his father, a well-known muralist, and his mom, a pianist. He has said he takes inspiration from his surrounding environments. He still remembers details about the Mexican streets he walked from home to school, including puddles and even sidewalk accidents. He once told the *New York Times*, "I want to be a kid. To keep making art, you have to put yourself in the position of a beginner. You have to be excited by a stone on the sidewalk or, like a child, the flight of a bird."

To spark this excitement, he still roams streets to observe his surroundings. He prefers this to working in an artist's studio, tucked away from the outside world. Art, to him, is about our relationship with the world. Gabriel has also used all sorts of things to make art: deflated footballs, abandoned kites, yogurt lids, games, cars, clay, Astroturf, a whale skeleton, and even toilet paper! He truly inspires people to reconsider the objects around us daily.

Although Gabriel doesn't specifically call himself an environmental artist, his work clearly demonstrates the negative impact humans have had on the world. Many artists prefer to let viewers decide what their work is supposed to mean. Gabriel's art challenges people to think

about the critical issues of the day and potential solutions for tomorrow. Scientists, activists, politicians, and businesspeople are obviously all needed in the climate fight. But artists who can change the way people see the world are uniquely important, and so are you.

IN 1994, GABRIEL married Maria Gutiérrez, who became a climate change expert for the United Nations.

IF YOU'RE INTERESTED in environmental art and how it can provoke people to think and take action, check out the Danish Icelandic artist Olafur Eliasson, who has displayed ice that broke off from Iceland's largest glacier. There's also the British artist John Sabraw, who uses toxic pollution to create his paint colors. And look into Paulo Grangeon, a French sculptor who created 1,600 papier-mâché panda bears he displays in many cities around the world to show how few pandas there are left on earth. Sadly, at this point, he may have made too many.

ACT LIKE GABRIEL

Use art to spark an environmental conversation about reusing and reducing waste. Collect garbage in your neighborhood, rinse it off, and make something with it! Invite your parents and friends to see your creations—and start talking.

KEN YEANG

B. 1948

Ecologist & Architect

Try a little experiment: The next time you walk down a street, take a close look at the buildings on it. Whether you're in a city with tall skyscrapers or a country road dotted with houses, consider what it took to build them. Then think about all it takes to maintain a house—from water to electricity—and also just keeping buildings warm or cool. Architect Ken Yeang has spent his entire career doing just this, thinking critically about all aspects of buildings and how they impact the earth, then building better ones that use earth-friendlier materials and require less energy and water. Ken's award-winning "green" (a.k.a. environmentally friendly) buildings can be found all over the world, including a library in Singapore and a children's hospital in London.

You know Ken's buildings are different the minute you see them, because they don't look like anything else—except maybe a drawing in a Dr. Seuss book! First of all, they usually have plants all over them. Some of them appear almost fuzzy because there are so many plants! It's as if Ken has blended nature with architecture. And in a sense, he has. What you can't tell just by looking at one of his buildings is that they're complete ecosystems designed specifically to use little outside energy. The places and even angles they're built on are chosen to allow wind in to cool and air out the buildings. The plants aren't just there because they're pretty and fun to look at; they filter air and clean wastewater. Ken has said building this way is the morally correct thing to do. We are living in a world of limited resources, and building carefully protects these resources for future generations.

Ken almost didn't become an architect. His father was a doctor and wanted him to be one, too. He visited his first construction site when he was four years old—a family house his father had built in Malaysia, where he grew up. The experience stuck with him and inspired him to be an architect.

Years later, in 1984, Ken built his own house based on his green design concepts. He named it Roof Roof. To keep Roof Roof cool in a tropical climate, he used special shades to block the hot morning sun and to create afternoon shelter. He also placed Roof Roof in a spot on the property where wind would blow over a pool, cooling the air before it entered the house. After experimenting on Roof Roof, he was able to use these ideas for his clients' buildings, too.

The climate crisis means many industries are now trying to go green—to keep doing what their work requires but operating in more earth-friendly ways. Building construction, which has a huge environmental impact, has been pretty slow to go green. Ken is his industry's inspiring leader. His "bioclimatic" designs are the most complete and thoughtful approach to green building anyone has come up with yet. Truly green buildings can have a tremendous positive effect and go a long way to protecting our earth. The more architects and people in the construction industry adopt Ken's ideas, the bigger the impact!

WHILE KEN'S WORK is serious, he can joke, too! He has been known to say, "As Kermit the Frog of *Sesame Street* says, 'It's not easy being green!'"

KEN ISN'T THE only architect in his family. Three of his uncles are also architects—he studied at a school one of them also attended.

ACT LIKE KEN

Ken has said he's an ecologist first and an architect second. Be an ecologist first in all you do! Prioritize clean air, water, and soil. Even if you're not building a skyscraper for a big company, do what you can in your own home to protect these limited and precious resources. If your parents are doing a home improvement project, talk to them about using greener materials—from paint to insulation.

EILEEN FISHER

B. 1950

Fashion Designer & Sustainable Business Leader

You love your favorite clothes because they fit well and look good. But have you ever considered their environmental impact? Probably not! It turns out that the fashion industry, according to some studies, is the second-largest polluter in the world. (The first is the oil industry.)

It doesn't seem possible that clothes could be as bad as fossil fuels, but fashion uses a lot of resources, and clothing manufacturing involves tons of harmful chemicals. Synthetic fabrics are even made from fossil fuels! Making cotton clothing—from jeans to leggings to sweatshirts—requires pesticides and fertilizers to grow the cotton, lots of water, and hazardous dyes, which pollute even more water. Even doing your laundry at home increases your clothing's **eco-footprint,** especially if you use energy to heat the water in your washing machine, detergents containing unsafe chemicals (which go into wastewater and wind up harming fish), and more energy to dry them. It's a complex problem that many of us are contributing to without knowing it just by getting dressed.

Fashion designer Eileen Fisher has been thinking deeply about this entire system of clothing—from fabrics to manufacturing to how her customers use her clothes—for decades. Sustainability wasn't on her mind when she launched her simple fashion line in 1984, but shortly after, she started researching every single step of what it takes to produce clothing, trying to make her brand as sustainable as possible.

With similar thought and effort, any business can change the world for the better. That's Eileen's goal. Today, her fabrics are organic, sustainable, and carefully purchased from eco-friendly companies. Eileen says she uses the least toxic fabric dyes she can find. Her brand manufactures some clothing in the United States, where environmental regulations for factories are stricter than in other countries. There's a person at her company who monitors environmental impact and looks for new ways to do everything more sustainably. One thing that really concerns Eileen is how much water is used for clothing—she says it takes about seven hundred gallons of water to make one T-shirt! Think about how many T-shirts you own, including the ones you get as soccer uniforms or birthday party favors that you'll never even wear. What a waste!

Eileen's passion is circular design. This means that instead of making clothes out of new materials and throwing them out when you're "done" with them (that's a straight line), she designs clothes for today that can become materials for "new" clothing tomorrow (that's a circle). The ultimate goal of circular design is reusing everything and adding zero waste to our landfills. To accomplish this, Eileen remanufactures her own clothing: her brand collects and resells used garments. Clothes that can't be resold get reused into totally new items. If you can't picture what that means, look on the company's website for cool examples!

Eileen's brand is a great model for anyone in the fashion industry. She's leading by example, proving there are awesome solutions available for designers and clothing companies to drastically reduce fashion's enormous eco-impact. The more brands that are inspired to follow her lead, the bigger the impact will be. She's also inspiring consumers to do their part and buy from earth-friendly labels. It's as simple as deciding you want to buy a better T-shirt or pair of pants. That's called voting with your dollars.

EILEEN'S COMPANY TAKES back clothing from her customers in any condition—holes, stains, whatever! These are repaired and resold, or if an item is in really bad shape, it's turned into scraps that are used to create something entirely new. The brand says it has already taken back 41,100,000 pieces of clothing!

SUSTAINABILITY ISN'T ONLY about saving water and using better fabric dyes. It's about personal sustainability, too. That's why Eileen pays her employees a fair amount of money and shares social ideas, too. For example, people with jobs at her company are encouraged to do volunteer work.

ACT LIKE EILEEN

Use fashion to make a statement that goes beyond being trendy! Shop for clothes made from organic cotton and other earth-friendlier materials. Or, to avoid the concerns of modern clothing manufacturing entirely, wear reused or vintage clothing.

133

ANOHNI

B. 1971

Singer & Environmentalist

There's a long history of musicians who create protest music for the issues of the day. Anohni has said artists have different responsibilities at different times. That's why she's currently writing and singing about the climate crisis. After years of singing about emotions and feelings with her band, Antony & the Johnsons, Anohni changed her name from Antony Hegarty, her pronoun from he to she, and transitioned her music as well. She released an album called *Hopelessness*, with songs about politics and current events, especially environmental disaster.

Anohni was born and spent her early years in England. She has memories of her father carrying her on his shoulders walking along the downs, which are grassy hills in Southern England. Her family also lived in Holland, then moved to California when she was ten. She has described herself as a creative kid, always working on all kinds of projects. At nineteen, she moved to New York City and began her unique career. She has won many awards for her work, and her fans and music critics alike are entranced by her angelic and unusual voice. It's hard to describe— give her songs a listen!

The night before the 2015 UN Climate Change Conference, where global leaders signed the Paris Climate Agreement, Anohni released a song from *Hopelessness* called "4 Degrees." The lyrics describe what would happen if the global temperature rises by 4 degrees Celsius— as some studies suggest it could by the end of the century if greenhouse gas emissions continue to go up the way they have been. Anohni sings hauntingly that "only" four degrees would mean the world will boil, the sky and the breeze will burn, and fish, lemurs, rhinos, and other creatures big and small will die. The *Guardian* newspaper called *Hopelessness* "the most profound protest record in decades."

Sadness about mass extinction, a changing environment, and a collapsing ocean weave through the songs on *Hopelessness*. Anohni has struggled with what she wants and hopes for our earth and our future while still being a member of modern society, which is addicted to burning fossil fuels for energy. How can we protest and talk about taking action to save plants and animals and to reduce emissions, but continue to fly in polluting airplanes, drive gas-guzzling cars, and do so many other things that are destroying the planet? We're contradicting ourselves.

Anohni uses her music to work through this struggle with honesty. We're all pointing fingers at who is responsible for the climate crisis, when really we're all to blame. Her lyrics make us look at our own roles—what we do as well as what we don't do. Although there are plenty of climate activists suggesting solutions, there aren't many asking people to confront reality the way Anohni does. She has made the climate crisis personal, placing huge issues in context and pushing us to consider our own responsibility as part of this global problem. Sometimes her songs can be scary or upsetting, but ultimately they're an amazingly beautiful call to arms.

ANOHNI HAS WORKED with many well-known musicians including Björk, Yoko Ono, and Lou Reed.

MULTITALENTED ANOHNI CONTINUES to be involved in many projects, just like when she was a kid. She's also a visual artist, and her drawings have been in galleries, shows, and museums all over the world.

ACT LIKE ANOHNI

Art can be a powerful way to share your concern about our earth. So sing a song, write a story, or paint a painting—use art to express yourself and inspire others to environmental action.

DAVID ATTENBOROUGH   B. 1926

Naturalist & Broadcaster

If you've ever watched a nature show with your family or at school, like a documentary about a certain species or about the plants and animals of Africa, there's a good chance Sir David Attenborough made it. Sir David has been making shows and documentaries about nature since the 1950s, mostly for the British Broadcasting Corporation (BBC). Sir David's interest in the natural world started at a young age; as a kid he was into collecting specimens and fossils and studying biology. He went on to study natural sciences at Cambridge University.

Even in the 1950s and 1960s, Sir David began noticing that humans were damaging the environment and that animal species were going extinct as a result. It took years for scientists to study and catch up to what Sir David was witnessing. Meanwhile, he educated countless people about nature, showing them on film just how exciting, beautiful, and important it is. He introduced television audiences to species never seen before, and he inspired many environmentalists, first with a series called *Zoo Quest* and then through many other shows like *Life on Earth, The Living Planet, The Trials of Life, Life in the Freezer* (that one is about Antarctica), *The Life of Birds, State of the Planet,* and *The Life of Mammals.* Sir David has a distinct style—he combines big sweeping images of nature and animals with voice-overs. He doesn't often appear on screen himself. Because of this, his voice—deep, slow, and with a British accent—is as famous as his documentaries and series.

Human impact on the natural world has become more and more obvious over the decades Sir David has spent documenting wildlife. His programs have reflected this change. They now cover melting glaciers and the loss of biodiversity—that means how many different plants and animals there are. In 2017, his documentary series *Blue Planet II* showed plastic pollution destroying marine life. In 2019, a Netflix series, *Our Planet,* offered suggestions on how the world can protect its ecosystems. He also made *Climate Change–The Facts,* which was on the BBC in 2019. In 2020, he released *A Life on Our Planet* about his amazing and long career as a naturalist.

In his ninth decade on earth, Sir David said that the future of civilization depends on how we respond to climate change. Throughout his many years of work, he was lucky to see so

many plants and animals in the wild. Those currently becoming extinct were created over billions of years of evolution. Sir David thought it wasn't right that modern people could destroy this in only a few decades. The man who taught generations to love our earth has also encouraged us to work with nature rather than against it and to act on the climate crisis now before it's too late.

· ·

THERE ARE SEVERAL species named after Sir David: a dinosaur (the attenborosaurus), a butterfly, an extinct grasshopper, a 430 million-year-old fossil, and more!

IN ENGLAND, YOU can be "knighted" by the queen for doing something great. In 1985, David was knighted for his wilderness programs. That's why he has the title *Sir* David Attenborough.

ACT LIKE DAVID

· ·

If you love nature, you're more likely to protect it. Today, many people live in cities and don't have a direct connection to nature. If you can't see frogs or hawks in your own backyard, take a family hike in a park near you and fall in love.

VANESSA HAUC

B. 1975

Journalist & Environmentalist

Journalists do important work all over the world. They find and share the news everyone needs to know, even when it's difficult to report and the truth can be hard to hear. Vanessa Hauc, a television journalist for Telemundo, a US-based Spanish-language media company, has reported on many topics over her career, but currently she's focusing on the environment—the most important story today.

Vanessa has seen the impact of climate change in person as a journalist. She has reported on the stronger storms, bigger fires, earthquakes, and devastating floods our warming planet is experiencing. A lot of the environmental news stories today are in English despite the fact that Latinx and minority communities are the most affected by the climate crisis. Vanessa fills this void by reporting in Spanish, the fourth-most-spoken language in the world! She educates and engages Telemundo's audience in America and beyond about the environment. She does this through her environmental news unit, Planet Earth (Planeta Tierra), and also through a program she hosts called *Green Alert (Alerta Verde),* where she explains environmental issues, making what's sometimes confusing a lot easier to understand. She also shares easy ways people can protect our planet.

Vanessa was born in Colombia. She moved to the United States to study communications and journalism at the University of Nevada. Now when hurricanes and wildfires hit Latinx American communities in places like Florida, Texas, and California, or when hurricanes hit Puerto Rico, Vanessa's there, reporting live.

Vanessa has seen the ways our changing climate has motivated people to come together to create a more sustainable future. She has witnessed this through years of work with Vice President Al Gore and his Climate Reality Project. Once a year, the project broadcasts "24 Hours of Reality," a full day of television devoted to telling the truth about the climate crisis and discussing its solutions. People all over the world, including Vanessa, make live presentations. In 2018, 800 million people tuned in!

In Spanish—and in English—Vanessa has educated countless people about the crisis and also the fixes that are right in front of us, interviewed the most important people in the environmental movement, and moved the global climate conversation forward. Political and government action are critical, but individual people must do their part, too. It's up to us to turn the tide! Vanessa is here to inform us and show us all the way.

VANESSA, AN EMMY Award–winning journalist, was named "one of the ten Latinos leading on climate" by the *Huffington Post*. In 2020, she was the first climate journalist ever to moderate a presidential debate.

VANESSA COFOUNDED AN organization called Sachamama to educate and inspire the Latinx community on climate issues and sustainability. *Sachamama* is Quechua (a language spoken in the Amazon and South American Andes) for "Mother Jungle."

ACT LIKE VANESSA

Report on the environment! Join your school newspaper, make a podcast, or start a YouTube channel to share stories about the environment in whatever language you speak and with whatever audience you think needs to hear it most. You might not have a Telemundo-sized audience, but you will make a difference!

YANN ARTHUS-BERTRAND

B. 1946

Aerial Photographer & Environmentalist

The earth has been around for a very long time—4.5 billion years, in fact. Humans have only been around for a tiny fraction of that time, but we've still managed to change the planet drastically for the worse. And in the past fifty years, we've altered it more completely than in the whole history of humanity. Humans depend on water, forests, deserts, and oceans. Now water is running low, half of the world's forests are gone, our energy sources aren't sustainable, and modern industrial farming is ruining our soil. We have changed our home. We know this, but we prefer not to believe it—this is called climate denial. Photographer Yann Arthus-Bertrand's striking pictures show humans' impact on the earth so clearly that we can no longer deny it. He makes us see the truth.

Yann is an aerial photographer, which means he takes pictures and video from the sky, usually from a helicopter. He's best known for his films, *Home* and *Human,* and especially for his book, *Earth from Above,* which came out in 1999. To this day, he stages free outdoor exhibitions of large photographs from *Earth from Above* in cities all over the world to raise awareness about the state of the planet. He estimates that about 200 million people have seen the exhibits.

Animals led Yann to nature photography. At age twenty, he became the director of a French nature reserve. At thirty, he and his wife studied a family of lions for three years in the Masai Mara reserve in Kenya. He took pictures to observe this pride, and he calls these lions his first photography teachers. To earn money, he became a hot air balloon pilot, which is also how he began taking aerial pictures and discovering the earth from above. Next he became a reporter focusing on environmental issues. Inspired by attending the 1992 Earth Summit in Rio, Brazil, as a journalist, Yann decided to merge his work and interests by photographing the entire planet from above. He spent years flying above sixty countries across five continents, capturing never-before-seen images and details. *Earth from Above* was the result.

Yann's images are gorgeous; he loves this planet and wants to show its beauty. But if you look closely, you can also see environmental destruction. A picture of palm tree plantations in Borneo shows deforestation. A shot of a beautiful reef illustrates how coral, so important for ocean plants and animals, is being wiped out because of global warming. A photo of the North Pole shows a new waterway where solid ice used to be. Another shot reveals Mt. Kilimanjaro, Africa's highest mountain, without its usual ice cap (it melted).

Home, which came out in 2009, highlights the depleted state of the planet. In the trailer, Yann says, "We haven't yet understood that we're going at a much faster pace than the planet can sustain." The film shows what we are losing and also what we can do about it. Maybe the most amazing thing about *Home* is not the movie itself but that Yann released it for free. Anyone can download and watch it. According to Yann, more than 600 million people have seen and shared *Home* so far and been educated about the climate crisis and its solutions—an incredible accomplishment!

YANN SET UP an organization, the Good Planet Foundation, to teach the world about environmental problems. Good Planet also fights deforestation and works on ways to reduce carbon emissions.

NOT MANY PEOPLE get into helicopter crashes and live to tell their stories. But in 2005, Yann did just that! His helicopter went down while he was filming the aftermath of Hurricane Katrina, which flooded the city of New Orleans. Thankfully, he survived.

ACT LIKE YANN

Yann says the best action you can take for the earth is to stop eating meat, especially industrially raised meat. If you eat meat, eat less meat, and ideally only meat that has been raised ethically and responsibly.

CHAI JING

B. 1976

Reporter & Filmmaker

What's the first thing you do in the morning? When Chai Jing wakes up, she checks the air pollution level on her phone. Smog is so bad in many parts of China that it's making people sick. Chai's goal is to protect her young daughter from breathing smog directly. So, on high pollution days in Beijing, where she lives, she keeps her indoors "like a prisoner." In 2014, there were 175 high-pollution days in Beijing—that's nearly half the year! Can you imagine not being allowed to go outside basically every other day because the air is not safe?

Chai has been researching Chinese air pollution for a long time. Her documentary about it, *Under the Dome,* got hundreds of millions of views in about a week when it was released online in 2015. The groundbreaking film made many people aware of the smog problem and how it was harming human health. It was compared to Rachel Carson's *Silent Spring,* the book that set off the American environmental movement. Unfortunately, after a week, the Chinese government, which controls what their citizens read and watch, blocked further viewing of *Under the Dome*. They apparently didn't want people to know about smog—where it's from, why it's bad, or how to keep from getting sick.

In *Under the Dome,* Chai speaks with many pollution experts, but one of the most interesting interviews is with a young girl. This girl only knows smog; she has never seen a real star, white clouds, or a totally blue sky. Chai worries that her daughter's life will be similar. Part of why she made the film is to explain to her child why she's kept indoors and what smog is.

Smog is basically tiny airborne particles of substances including toxic chemicals known to cause health problems like cancer. Smog comes mainly from burning fossil fuels—like dirty coal for electricity and oil that we burn as gasoline when we drive cars and trucks. China burns a lot of coal and has a lot of traffic, which has resulted in their big smog problem.

The particles in smog get into human bodies when we breathe and make us ill. Chai describes her throat pain and chronic coughing in her film. The smaller your lungs are, the more smog can damage your health, so it's particularly bad for kids. "Each of us is living our lives in an experiment chamber," Chai says in the film.

Under the Dome shares scary statistics, like the fact that 500,000 people die because of air pollution every year. Chai says that in the past thirty years in China, death by lung cancer has increased by a huge amount. Many citizens don't know wearing masks and using air filters can help protect them from smog. Plus, not everyone can afford to buy them.

Smog is bad, but it can be reversed. The solutions, like not using coal as a main source of energy, are obvious. Some big cities, like London and Los Angeles, have been able to drastically reduce their pollution. China, thanks in part to Chai, may follow their lead. Even though the Chinese government blocked *Under the Dome*, Chai started an important national discussion about air pollution. You can't hide smog, even if you ban an investigative film about it! Chai has dedicated her life to uncovering the truth, risking censorship to make the world a better place—for her daughter and everyone in China.

DEPENDING ON WHAT country you live in, you can watch all of or parts of *Under the Dome* online with subtitles, even though it has been banned in China. Just Google it!

HERE ARE SOME tips inspired by *Under the Dome* to help reduce air pollution no matter where you live:

1. Ride a bike for transportation.
2. Ask your parents not to let your car engine idle. Have your school set up a "no idling zone" for pickup and drop-off.
3. Have your parents report any diesel trucks releasing black smoke.
4. Enlist your family to boycott products that come from polluting manufacturers.
5. Talk to family members about ways to demand strong air pollution laws and enforcement.

ACT LIKE CHAI

Speak up! Even if your government tries to hide the truth, spread the word in whatever way you can to protect yourself and teach others how to protect themselves from harm.

DAVID SUZUKI   B. 1936

Science Broadcaster & Environmental Activist

When David Suzuki was a kid in Vancouver, Canada, he spent time camping and fishing with his father. He grew up to become a well-known scientist and Canadian television host. By the time his grandkids asked him to take them fishing where he had gone as a child, he couldn't—there were no more fish in that spot. That's how much the environment changed in David's lifetime.

David studied biology at college, got a PhD in zoology at the University of Chicago, and then returned to Canada to teach in 1961. He spent one year at the University of Alberta and then moved to the University of British Columbia, where he was a professor from 1963 to 2001, specializing in genetics. While at the University of Alberta, David made an on-campus television show. He had never watched television growing up, and, at that point, he didn't even own a TV! But the experience made him realize TV was a great way to educate lots of people about science—it could be a powerful tool for good.

He started using this powerful tool by reviewing science books for the Canadian Broadcasting Corporation (CBC) and eventually wound up with a regular show, *Suzuki on Science*. Today, people have access to tons of TV channels, but in the early 1970s, the CBC was the main channel in Canada (sometimes the only channel, depending on where you lived). David became a media personality: Canada's national science guide. He made science easy for people to understand and went on to have many other shows, including *Quirks and Quarks* on the CBC's radio station. In 1979, he started hosting the long-running television show *The Nature of Things*. He also hosted many specials, including *A Planet for the Taking*.

Through his TV and radio work, David grew increasingly aware of and began to report on our changing climate. After he hosted an environmentally themed 1988 radio series called *It's a Matter of Survival*, thousands of people wrote letters asking him what they could do to help. In response, David and his wife set up the David Suzuki Foundation to protect nature and to inspire Canadians to act with it in mind. David has gotten many awards for his years of dedication to the earth, including a UN Environment Program medal.

David has overcome many trials in his life, including racism. He has been honored for trying to help Canada's Indigenous people protect their ancestral land from environmentally harmful projects like oil pipelines. He's an inspiration.

Late in his career, David started cutting back on travel in an effort to reduce greenhouse gas emissions from flying and driving to conferences and speaking engagements. David has said he's neither an optimist nor a pessimist about the climate crisis and our future, but he believes no one has the right to say it's too late to fix what's broken. These are wise words for all from a science guide as we head toward an uncertain future!

DAVID IS A prolific writer! He has written or coauthored more than fifty books—and almost twenty of those are for kids.

A FILM MADE about David, *Force of Nature: The David Suzuki Movie,* won a People's Choice documentary award at the 2010 Toronto International Film Festival.

ACT LIKE DAVID

Study science, especially climate science, and educate people about what you have learned. You may not have a show on CBC, but you can make your own podcast or YouTube videos and get involved with your school newspaper.

GLOSSARY

Here are a few important environmental terms that come up a lot in the prior pages—and what they mean.

BIODIVERSITY

The huge variety of life on earth is biodiversity. It's a broad term, encompassing every living thing on our planet, even bacteria. As our environment changes for various reasons, including the climate crisis, we are losing its biodiversity as certain plants and animals are going extinct. But the word can be used more narrowly, too. When we cut down trees in a specific forest, you lose the biodiversity of the plants and animals that lived in that particular place.

CLIMATE CHANGE AND CLIMATE CRISIS

A change in climate means that average conditions of things like temperature or the amount of rain or snow in a specific region—a city or a state or even a country—have shifted over time. Scientists have been observing that the temperature at the earth's surface is currently warming. Over the past few decades, they have recorded the warmest seasons and years ever. This change is now being called a crisis because it is causing melting glaciers, sea level rise, and loss of biodiversity, including what humans rely on for food—all things that will make the earth an increasingly difficult place to inhabit.

CLIMATE JUSTICE

Research has shown that certain people, including communities of color, are more likely to experience the effects of climate change than others. Often the people most affected are the least responsible for causing the problem. This is unfair. Rich countries are more responsible for the climate crisis—people who live in them use more resources, fly in airplanes more often, drive their cars more, and so on—and yet poor developing countries are suffering more from the climate crisis. Climate justice means addressing the climate crisis and trying to even out what's unbalanced or unfair in terms of human rights at the same time.

CONTAMINATION

There are many ways humans pollute the environment. When we spray chemicals like pesticides on our crops, they make their way into our waterways. When those chemicals get into our water, they pollute—or contaminate—it and the animals and plants that live in it. That is just one kind of contamination. We contaminate the air when we burn certain fossil fuels. We contaminate the water when plastic bottles and garbage end up in our oceans. And so on.

DEFORESTATION

When humans cut down large areas of trees to use the land for something else, that's deforestation. Cutting down trees to clear land for whatever reason—logging, construction, cattle ranching, farming, mining, agriculture—has a huge negative impact on wildlife, soil, water, air, and the people who live near and depend on the forest. Large-scale deforestation of the world's biggest rain forests has been linked to the climate crisis.

ECO-FOOTPRINT OR ECO-IMPACT

This term refers to how much something you buy or use—from your jeans to your family's car—harms or helps the earth. Every single thing on earth, including you, has an impact on the environment. Something like an organic carrot has positive eco-impact, or very little footprint, while taking an airplane to a far-away destination has negative eco-impact, or bigger footprint.

FOSSIL FUEL

Petroleum, coal, and natural gas are all fossil fuels. They're actually the remains of plants and animals that lived a long time ago. But just because they're natural does not mean they are good for us to use. Taking fossil fuels out of the earth then refining and transporting them for consumer use is an all-around eco-unfriendly process. Burning fossil fuels creates air pollution (which is bad for your health) and carbon pollution (which contributes to climate change). To slow the climate crisis, we must move away from global dependence on fossil fuels and adopt cleaner energy sources that constantly renew themselves, like solar and wind power.

GENETICALLY MODIFIED ORGANISMS (GMOS) AND GENETICALLY MODIFIED (GM) FOOD

These terms refer to plants that get artificially changed in laboratories as well as their resulting crops (things like vegetables, wheat, and fruit). These changes—or modifications—are done to make seeds and plants resistant to disease, insects, or viruses to increase the amounts of crops that can be grown. An example of genetic modification would be taking genes from bacteria, viruses, insects, or even chickens, and inserting them into a potato plant to make it stronger. Typical GM foods include corn and soy, both of which are ingredients in a wide variety of packaged foods like chips and breakfast cereal. Though some safety research has been conducted, there's still a lot of concern in the scientific and food communities about the health and environmental effects of GM food, which is why the USDA doesn't allow them to be labeled organic. Many other countries have banned genetically modified foods entirely because of safety questions.

GREENHOUSE GASES, THE GREENHOUSE EFFECT, AND GLOBAL WARMING

Have you ever been in a greenhouse in a plant nursery or store? It's always nice and warm in there. Think of the earth like a giant greenhouse. There are certain gases in the air, called greenhouse gases, that trap energy from the sun, and these help warm the earth's surface. This is called the greenhouse effect. Some of the gases trapping heat are water vapor, methane, and carbon dioxide. The earth actually needs the greenhouse effect; it makes it warm enough for humans to live here! But now certain things we are doing, like driving cars and burning coal at factories, have drastically increased the amount of greenhouse gases on earth, making it warmer than it should be. This added heat is why there has been a rise in temperature at the earth's surface—this is global warming, and it is triggering our climate crisis.

ORGANIC

When you see food labeled "organic" at a grocery store or a farmers' market, it has a very specific meaning. In the United States, "organic" is defined and regulated by the United States Department of Agriculture (USDA). Organic meat, poultry, and dairy products are guaranteed to be free of specific chemicals, hormones, and antibiotics, and the animals they come from aren't allowed to be kept in cramped cages or bad conditions. For fruits and vegetables, as well as packaged foods that contain them, "certified organic" means that no synthetic pesticides or fertilizers were used to grow them. They were grown with organic farming practices. Also, organic foods—and even the feed that organic meat and dairy animals eat—can't contain genetically modified ingredients.

RENEWABLE ENERGY

We all use energy every day for the electricity that lights our homes, charges our devices and cell phones, and so much more. When an energy source is renewable, this means you can replenish it. Reusing energy that's constantly created in our natural world from sources like the sun and the wind, which don't pollute our air or water or make our planet warmer, is good common sense. It's also eco-friendly. Fossil fuels, on the other hand, are finite, which means they cannot be renewed. We have a set amount of them in the earth, and once we use them up, that's it—we won't have any more.

SINGLE-USE PLASTICS

There are certain plastics meant to be reused, and then there are others meant to be used once and then thrown away. Things like straws, food packaging, plastic forks, and grocery bags are often made of single-use plastic. Using something once and throwing it away is not eco-friendly, especially when you consider that a lot of plastic is made out of fossil fuels. What a waste! When we throw single-use plastics in the garbage after using them sometimes for only a few minutes, they either stick around in landfills basically forever, or they accidentally wind up in our oceans and contaminate the water. Marine life and fish also wind up eating plastics as the water breaks them down into smaller pieces. Reusable materials have a much better eco-impact and a smaller footprint than single-use plastics. There are straws made of glass and metal, glass containers for food, reusable forks, and cloth grocery bags. Choose them!

SUSTAINABLE/SUSTAINABILITY

These words get used a lot! Maybe you've heard people talk about sustainable farming or your favorite clothing company has said it's working on sustainability. Something that's sustainable can be done for as long as is wanted without harming the environment or using up natural resources, especially those that cannot be renewed. Sustainable farming tends to be organic or natural—it doesn't harm the soil, so it can be done for a good, long while. When a company is working on sustainability, that means it is trying to use better ingredients and manufacturing processes that will be safe long term.

155

ACKNOWLEDGMENTS

To my family—immediate and extended—especially to Olli for reading every word I've ever written (more than once). To Aili and Lyyli for inspiration, tolerance of all things eco-friendly (sorry about "green" Halloween—sort of), and making it possible for me to even know how to explain what's arguably confusing in a clear way for all ages. To my dad (now Bapa Rog) for always eagle-eyeing my contracts. To Rica Allannic for years of eco-interest, a fun reunion, and a great idea. To Jess Riordan (and Harry, who arrived on the scene in the middle of Carrie Watterson's deft copyedit!) for giving *Earth Squad* a happy home. And to the whole Running Press Kids team: Marissa Raybuck, Valerie Howlett, my email buddy Julie Matysik, Kristin Kiser, and Cisca Schreefel. Thanks to Nhung Lê for making my wordy world come alive visually. I hope to get to meet you all in person one day! Halfway through the process of writing, editing, and proofreading these very pages, we all, like the rest of the world, needed to quarantine for global health. We were able to more or less seamlessly continue our work, so thanks also to the internet and email, plus WebEx, FaceTime, Google Hang, Zoom, and so on. Here's to a new amazing squad that came on all of our radars as we worked: the first responders and front-line workers who made it possible for us all to produce a book in the safety of our own homes. A global pandemic plus the Black Lives Matter revolution have a unique way of shining a spotlight on the climate crisis; may we all learn this lesson and join the movement to act on it with urgency. To every single member of the Earth Squad past and present; there are so many more of us doing this critical work, day in and day out, than the fifty brilliant warriors in these pages: Thank you. And, finally, to my readers: although it's not at all up to children alone to fix the environmental issues we face globally, we could really use your energy and your ideas. I am so glad you're here and want to be part of the Earth Squad. Let's get to work.

ABOUT THE AUTHOR

Alexandra Zissu is a proud member of the Earth Squad. She is a journalist and the author of the book *The Conscious Kitchen* and coauthor of *The Complete Organic Pregnancy, Planet Home, The Butcher's Guide to Well-Raised Meat,* and *Get on Top.* A native New Yorker, Alexandra now lives in the Hudson Valley with her family to be close to the farms and farmers that feed them. She loves family meals and finds pure magic in growing a small raised bed of peas, lettuces, cucumbers, ground cherries, cherry tomatoes, and herbs with her two daughters.

To act like Alexandra, you, too, can learn and write about environmental topics, ask everyone you know to take steps to go green, avoid plastic, spend lots of time in nature, support local farms, and plant (organic) seeds. If you're having trouble taking an Earth Squad action, want encouragement, or ever have a question, head to AlexandraZissu.com to get in touch!

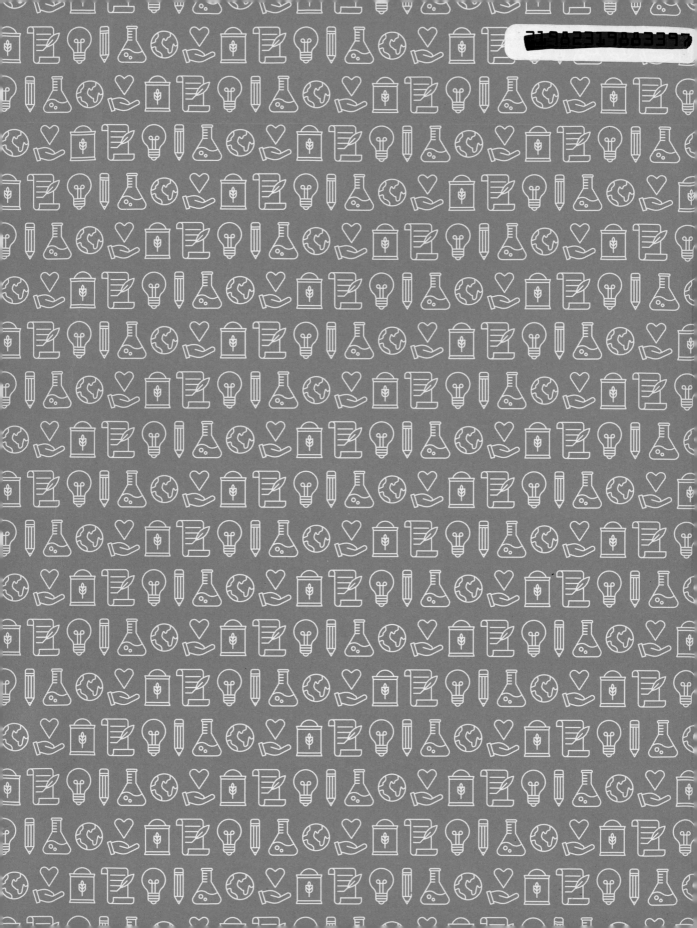